Perverse and Foolish

Perverse
and
Foolish

A Memoir of Childhood
and Youth

L.M. BOSTON

THE BODLEY HEAD
LONDON SYDNEY
TORONTO

British Library Cataloguing
in Publication Data
Boston, Lucy Maria
Perverse and foolish.
1. Boston, Lucy Maria – Biography
2. Authors, English – 20th century – Biography
I. Title
823'.9'14   PR6052.078z/
ISBN   0-370-30184-6

Printed in Great Britain for
The Bodley Head Ltd
9 Bow Street, London WC2E 7AL
by Redwood Burn Ltd, Trowbridge & Esher
Set in Monotype Imprint 101
by Gloucester Typesetting Co Ltd
First published 1979

To Peter and Diana Gunn
who with their curiosity and
expectation—of what?—
positively drove me, unwilling,
to write this book

ILLUSTRATIONS

Foreword

I have no guarantee of what is written here but memory, a known cheat. Looking back from my eighty-fifth year there is much that has faded out altogether, but here and there at random, pictures clear and bright as the magic lantern slides of my childhood stand out, which I must believe. Nobody else need! The chronology has slipped, before and after often get mixed. I have tried to keep a continuous story and to amplify it as little as possible with hindsight. I remember and have put down the thoughts and feelings as they were then, not as later experiences would recreate them.

L.M.B.

I

My earliest memory is of sitting in front of the nursery fire-guard in the evening beside the feet and blue-calico-covered knees of Nurse, with my youngest brother in a crib close by. The room was big and full of shadows that flopped in the jumping fire light. I was seized with a sudden rash feeling of adventure. I would cross the mysterious room right to the other side. I crawled as far as the table and under it, and then the great loneliness of so much empty shadowed space frightened me and I hurried back to those familiar knees. This one odd picture in my mind is dated by the fact that I was still crawling, but I seem to have been as much myself as I am now. At least in memory no difference is perceptible.

The nursery was in fact abnormally big. My father was an eccentric with big ideas, a small, goodhumoured, dynamic man. I was said to be strikingly like him, though I can't see it in photos, or in the very unappealing portrait of him as Mayor that confronted all my youth. It was a monstrous picture, painted by a cripple (doubtless because he was a Wesleyan as we all were) *with his feet*. None of the family portraits were masterpieces, but the older they were the better. This one, though competent and immensely present, was repulsive. The sitter was wearing the gold Mayoral chain of which the medallion rested on a tight round belly. His trousers also were tight and on each knee rested, Ramesses-like, a podgy hand. I used to try to feel love and admiration for the parent so presented for my consideration, grim-mouthed and blankly glaring, but it could not be done.

However, much later on, Stanley Spencer, who had become a close friend of my brother James, greatly admired a photograph of Father and used it for the figure of God in his great Resurrection picture in the Tate.

My grandfather Peter Wood was better represented by a marble bust that, mounted on an apricot marble column, dominated our dining room. This we all admired, and my brother James at the end of his life greatly resembled it. Peter Wood was a physician who had taken up the new idea of sea bathing for health. He chose the safe and sandy beach of Southport, then quite undeveloped, and built a row of charming little Regency houses on the front to be rented by his patients. The sea has retreated from Southport. Even in my childhood it was often out of sight. The Promenade and the Marine Drive were built one after the other to fill the stretch of sand as the sea withdrew. The little houses, if they still exist, are lost in the seething vulgarity of the present town.

I never knew any of my grandparents. On the Wood side they had eight daughters before my father was born, and one son after him. All the family were passionate Wesleyans and their passion gave them dignity. My grandfather promoted the building, on half of his own garden, of a very big chapel, of which the architecture, smell and stencilled decoration are forever imprinted on me, horrible, but redeemed by the curiosity, interest and irrepressible humour of a pewful of children whose legs did not reach the floor. From the Chapel grounds a Gothic arch in the wall gave private entrance to the family residence. It gave also a certain creepiness to that end of the garden as I always imagined coffin after coffin carried through it. In fact, of course, however short the distance funerals would have been carried out in state with hearse and broughams from one pillared gate and in at another fifty yards away.

Grandfather had lived in considerable style in a large house called 'Woodbank' set in about ten acres. As a child I used to see the family coach in the coach house, incredibly dusty, woodworm- and moth-eaten, standing with raised shafts, too forgotten even to be wanted out of the way.

The house was then inhabited by three unmarried aunts. My father was well over forty when he married, so his elder sisters were old ladies when we were children. One had remained a nightmare figure for life. She was the eldest, known to us as Beady Liz. We used to meet her drawn in a Bath chair by a decrepit old man (doubtless a Wesleyan) round her garden. She wore a bonnet of jet with black antennae, a black cloak trimmed with jet arabesques, and in her pinched face her eyes were jet. She sat upright and rigid in her ludicrous hooded vehicle like an upended coffin, showing no sign of life but hostility, and took the air in this fashion round her own grounds in solitary repudiation of the wicked world. There was also at times a widower-in-law, a tall, tottering zombie who qualified for Monty James' scholar whose eye-sockets were covered with cobwebs. To stop and say, 'Good morning, Uncle Jenkins' to him was more than a child dared.

The youngest of Father's sisters, Emily, also lived there but I do not remember her till somewhat later. She evidently could not get on with her sisters, for when she settled in, they moved out. She had avoided the invalidism of the others and was in fact something of a tartar, with eyebrows flying up into the roots of her hair and a habit of saying exactly what she thought. She dressed sumptuously in purple, and she mocked. The boys liked her. She could and did command the minister to come and pray with her when she wanted company, and having got him there flirted very effectively.

*

In order to be near the family home and its affiliated Chapel, my father took a house in the street which led directly to the double wrought-iron gates. It was a mean street of small, identical, barely genteel houses. Aunt Emily's companion

Miss Millington lived in one. I never knew of, even less met, any other inhabitant of the street. All the gardens contained privet and laurel. All the windows had Nottingham lace curtains well drawn across, with an aspidistra inside to block the central gap. My father having bought such a house began—in which I see my likeness to him—by knocking off the roof and the whole back of the house in order to double the depth and put on an extra storey. He built out a wing on one side and put in outsized bow windows on the whole front and back. It dominated the modest street. All this was in preparation for the family he intended to have. He then got craftsmen—well chosen—to paint all the important rooms to his requirements. The doors were painted in beautiful pastel colours with panels full of delicate flowers such as surround Persian miniatures. On ribbons among the flowers were moral maxims. These doors were done with such perfect workmanship that after thirty years of rackety family life the surface and colours were still most beautiful.

In the breakfast room above the picture rail a passage of Scripture travelled across three sides. It read, 'The lines are fallen unto me in pleasant places. Yea, I have a goodly heritage.' While one was stirring porridge one's eyes turned round the room to read it.

The long dining room had heavily carved beetling wooden mantels for the two fireplaces, and life-sized family portraits of four generations hung round. Above them a painted frieze gave place at regular intervals to mottos such as,

'He that giveth to the poor shall not lack.'
'Honour thy father and thy mother.'
'Thine own friend and thy father's friend forsake not.'
'The soul is not where it lives but where it loves.'

I used to know them all, but these were in view from my usual place at table and have sunk in. In the bedroom one could not stand to warm oneself by the fire without an exhortation to prayer staring at one from just below the mantelshelf, but the triumph of eccentricity was the drawing room. I wonder what my poor mother thought when first she saw it. This was where she was to entertain the Mayor's associates and friends. My father had recently been to the Holy Land and had brought much back with him, his idea being apparently to make a holy and uplifting room, perhaps such a room as Joseph of Arimathea might have had, or perhaps he was just letting his fancy have a fling. The frieze was a continuous painted landscape representing the journey from Jerusalem to Jericho. Under it the walls were divided into recesses by very intricate and beautifully made wooden arcades of the Moorish onion shape, a pattern unknown here. Who can he possibly have found to make them? Each recess was fitted with semi-circular seats covered with a material brought back for the purpose. It appeared to be woven of horse hair and metal and was like a file to the back of children's knees. It never wore out and never could. From the ceiling hung antique brass lamp-holders shaped like udders with glass oil-containers hanging down, such as might have hung in Solomon's temple. There were many beautiful objects made of brass beaten out almost as thin as linen: a life-sized cock with windblown tail feathers, a duck, a coffee jug with a spout like a swan's neck and a bowl to stand it in.

Other rarities were displayed in a glass-fronted cupboard made in the same fantastic elaboration as the recess. It was of natural black wood, very handsome. The lower half displayed a plaster facsimile of the Warning Stone from the temple of Solomon. The translation below read,

'Let no foreigner enter within the paling
Round the Holy Places and its precincts.
Now whosoever shall be taken therein
Shall be found guilty unto death.'

This unexpected room did not look at all like a Kardomah

Café as you might perhaps think. It looked like a gentleman's enthusiastic and satisfied near-lunacy. My mother had neither enthusiasm nor fantasy nor taste. She was totally indifferent to the appearance of things, but possibly not to the expression on visitors' faces. As they left the house they would read over the inside of the front door 'The Lord shall bless thy goings out and thy comings in'.

*

To return to the nursery in which the six of us lived. We were girl, boy, girl, boy, girl, boy at yearly intervals. I was the penultimate, between my brother Frank above and Phil below. Jamie (later known as Jas), dazzlingly handsome with huge brilliant eyes, was the god and tyrant of the tribe, but all were under the governorship of Nurse. It was she who brought us up. She was a big quiet woman, a disciplinarian whose command was never queried, but kind and fair. I can see the nursery table, all present, with Phil and myself in high chairs and Nurse unsmiling in charge. She was not a highly trained Norland Nurse, but a good serious Lancashire native. She had been, before Mother married, in her Sunday School class, and had come with her as a support and help in the new life.

Nurse disapproved of too much laughter at table, and frequently threatened that she would make us laugh on the other side of our faces, but she never slapped us. From the protected piety of my high chair, rather like a pulpit, I watched the way of the world. I saw with interest my sister Frances push the crust she had been told to eat down the tea-pot spout while Nurse was mopping up Phil. The sin would clearly come to light, and did. Frances was made to stand in the corner. This was Nurse's most severe punishment. I wonder how far back in nursery history standing in the corner goes, and what genius in child psychology first thought of it. I often saw Frances and Frank banished there and once stood there myself. I went defiant and unrepressed; there was an interesting super-cornerishness about the corner at first. One fitted it so neatly, and it offered a different slant of wall-paper to each eye. The pattern was repeated illustrations of 'Goosey, Goosey Gander', of which the upstairs and downstairs offered amusement as one covered first one eye and then the other. But very soon the corner became the most boring and constricting of prisons. One's back was blind and vulnerable and desolate, and all life was going on behind it. Jamie of course needed severer treatment. He was passionate and spoilt. Still in my high chair, waiting for the others to take their places, I once saw with shocked disapproval, that with his belt, of which the buckle was interlocking metal snakes, Jamie was slashing Frances. For this he was taken down to Father. In the study was kept a swishing cane, ornamented at the thick end with a crimson tassel. No doubt for thrashing his sister it was well applied. Frank was not yet old enough to have been caned, but regarded the implement with awe, especially the ritual tassel.

Nurse was totally loyal to our parents. Daily she told us of their virtues and notability. I do not think she was happy. All her meals were in the nursery at the top of the house, not personally brought her but sent up on a lift. She must have been lonely, perhaps more effaced than self-effacing. She attended the Salvation Army which perhaps was less cold than the Chapel where her station was rigidly marked out. She took us there, but did not even share the pew. In the evenings she picked out on a small Jew's harp the tunes of Moody and Sankey hymns, a most melancholy substitute for the music she had in her. All the training I ever had was from her, and yet I cannot recall a reprimand or a punishment, though she often looked very grim.

Our parents we saw once a day at Family Prayers, to which we were taken down. When we had all taken our seats on the chairs in front of which we should later kneel, the servants filed soberly in and sat in a row beside the door. Father then read from the big family Bible, sometimes making me stand between his knees while he guided my fat finger along under the words. (He called me his 'little Pige', short for pigeon.) Those of us who were old enough to memorise then said, in turn, a verse of Scripture. Phil at his first effort said with simplicity, 'He maketh me to lie down in still waters', which disturbed the gravity of the occasion, and thereafter he was never asked to try.

Strange to say, I remember nothing of the actual prayers, impromptu of course. Later on I had plenty of experience of very embarrassing prayers. Presumably Father's were short and in Biblical language. After Prayers we followed Father into his study on the first floor where we each received a small biscuit with a twirl of pink sugar on top, and were dismissed to the nursery. Very occasionally Father and Mother would come up to see us before we went to bed when we were larking around on the top landing. They laughed as if at a play, but only stayed a minute and never played with us. On Sundays of course there was Chapel, and after that we all, on our best manners, came down for Sunday dinner, always roast beef and Yorkshire pudding, followed by red and yellow jellies. Before the meal we all sang 'Praise God from whom all blessings flow', and after it 'We thank thee Lord for this our food'. In between these two verses we ate and absorbed the good words before our eyes on the frieze.

This was all that as small children we normally saw of our parents.

*

The nursery as I have said was very big, the size of three main rooms under it. Surprisingly it had no texts. Nurse evidently did not count. Of course she was not being brought up. The kitchen also was without, not even 'Blessed are the poor', but over the range in large letters, tersely, 'Waste not, want not'. I do not think that the texts were for ostentation, but rather that Father just felt happy among them.

In the nursery there was of course the old rocking horse, which after travelling round the family nurseries is now with me again. Father had ideas ahead of his time. He had had made a movable, detached flight of stairs as part of the nursery furniture. They were hollow underneath and easily housed all our toys, and provided a useful series of levels for many games. I chiefly remember sitting on the top step with a toy harp being an angel, a game with no holding power. The small wooden harps, with strings so loose they made no sound, were totally unpleasing: I wonder what misguided relative chose them for us. We had special toys for Sunday such as bricks that would only build chapels and Noah's arks. It was a limited range. We might have enjoyed missionaries and cannibals as a change from soldiers, but no one had thought of that. Sunday books were either uplifting or depressing— the New Testament illustrated in colour, very nightgowny, *Pilgrim's Progress* also illustrated, in which Apollyon, and even more Giant Despair, terrified me, and Foxe's *Book of Martyrs* with every kind of martyrdom vigorously depicted. On Sundays too we went down after tea to the crusaders' drawing room where we played 'Onward Christian Soldiers marching as to war' in and out of the small inlaid tables, singing as we went. The Persian carpet trodden by those infant feet is under my feet now. It gave one a shock after writing those words to look up and see it. Five pairs of those feet are gone.

The house was lit by gas which I remember most clearly in the bedrooms where we were after dark. There was a simple jet, unshaded, which gave a flat square flame, blue at the source and yellow at the top. What can possibly have lit that drawing room? I have an uncomfortable hazy feeling of pale blue fluted and flounced glass shades, ludicrous in that setting. Fairly early on a change was made to electric light, an exciting innovation; when I went to boarding school ten years later, they had still not caught up with it. The workmen were in the house a long time. We always enjoyed workmen who are generally so understanding with children. We were, I am sorry to say, provided with sheets of paper printed with texts in a particular lettering made up of broken bamboo sticks, for some reason special to texts, never seen in any other context. These we coloured with crayons and lovingly presented to the men. They were received with grins but never rejected. The electric wires were hidden under strips of wooden moulding up and down and round the rooms. The odd lengths left over we collected to make marble runs. Jamie was very ingenious at this, starting from the top of our movable flight of steps, with different gradients, angles, drops, tunnels and even see-saws. The various speeds, pauses and reverberations could make pleasing music as the marble obediently ran.

For weekdays we had many and splendid toys, especially Jamie, possibly chosen for the first-born son by an enthusiastic father. They added much to his kudos in my eyes. Phil and I, coming at the end, had nothing to compare with them. Mary and Frances too had superior dolls. Theirs were jointed all over, even their wrists and ankles, their bodies and limbs covered with white doe-skin, soft to touch. Their faces were china, not plastic, smooth to a young finger with a slight egg-shell drag. Their hair was real hair, their clothes hand-sewn with doll-sized stitches and tiny buttons, all complete, everything we wore. They were Victorian young ladies who did not smirk. Their eyelids closed over their eyes with real lashes. They had dignity and manners.

Every Saturday we were given one penny to spend as we chose. Nurse took us to the penny stall in the Market, where wonders could be bought, such as a gilded state coach two inches high with two horses, wheels that really went round and doors that opened, showing the seat inside, or 'silver' cups, saucers and teapot on a tiny 'silver' tray. The boys bought cannons, whistles or tops, or more often liquorice 'tram lines' that hung revoltingly out of their blackened mouths as they consumed them inch by inch. When in season I always bought a pansy root with one velvet flower, thrilled with the whole smell of wet paper, soil, leaf and pansy. As the soil of our garden was grey sand, almost nothing grew, but

Jamie had a white lupin which I thought a wonder from heaven. My father had made an attempt at laying out the small back garden which had high walls all round and no sun. It had sycamores, laurel and privet and one small rose, probably the old Monthly Rose as I do not remember any scent. This was the only rose of my childhood and I treasured it. It was set among rockery stone of some soft white substance like half-consolidated marble with crystal granulations. With a penknife one could scratch out caves in them and with the sand trickling round their bases they made a thrilling terrain for the mounted toy soldiers of the Boer War. We were Boer War children. We wore on our lapels buttons printed with the face of our preferred General—'Bob', Lord Roberts, being the most popular. We all knew and sang both the words and tunes of the war songs of the moment—'The Absent-Minded Beggar' and 'Oh! Listen to the Band'. One may wonder how, without radio or gramophone, a whole nation came to them; I suppose individually, each from the other like bees in a hive.

The sterility of this garden affected me from a very early age, and until I bought the Manor at Hemingford Grey forty odd years later my most recurrent dream was trying to reform that sixteenth of an acre of disappointment.

We had the run of the garden belonging to the Aunts. They kept two old gardeners and a gardener's boy. The Aunts were invalided indoors behind their bedroom curtains and as far as we could tell never looked out. The garden was kept severely decent.

I could still make an accurate map of all its paths and corners. It was interlaced with gravel walks which the gardener's boy on his knees weeded with finger and thumb month after month so that never a pebble had a blade of new grass beside it. The main pillared gates were opposite the end of our road, but inside them was a long drive, under a double row of trees, finally coming to a dead end. Probably, before he sacrificed half his garden to the Chapel, the affluent physician could drive across to a second gateway on the far side. The heavily draped main windows of the house looked over a long lawn in the middle of which stood a pedestalled urn with geraniums. Otherwise there were no flowers. Nobody went into the garden except ourselves. A doctor, of whom I am sure my sea-bathing grandfather would not have approved, was making a good living by persuading all wealthy ladies to take to their beds at the age of forty and remain there for life, seeing him constantly. My Aunts were therefore permanent invalids, only occasionally feeling well enough to take the air in a Bath chair, as I have described. Usually we had the place to ourselves and when we reached the bicycling age must have caused the old gardeners despair by rutting up the perfectly regulated pebbles of the paths. There was an orchard, the trees planted in naked beds with a path between them every six feet. Further away, screened from the gentry by a long artificial bank twelve feet high, was the kitchen garden, each bed hidden from sight by a dense privet hedge as if vegetables were indecent. In the high bank, as I scrambled up, I once saw a primrose and a cowslip. Someone in the far distant past, before the doctor cast his wicked spell, must have enjoyed this bank and planted it. Also once, by mistake, a tiger lily flowered by the old pump, last unvalued descendant of a living garden.

For us every path, every crossing or corner had a name. We cycled madly round, skidding as we turned. No wonder the withered gardeners were soured. Their tidy death of a garden was nevertheless the best thing in our home life. We were without any supervision and the labyrinth of paths was too extensive to be boring. The day before my schooldays were to begin, I wandered by myself in the Aunts' garden on a beautiful evening, looking at the golden sky and the poplars traced against it and lamenting that my life was now over for ever, never to be free again. I was seven. I think it was then that I began to realise that landscape was what moved me most. A few years later I knew it as both my anchorage and my motive force.

*

At home we met no other children but cousins. Only Wesleyans were fit company for us and unfortunately Methodism was a religion chiefly drawing tradesmen, except for a few leading families such as ours. The Wood family speech and manners were upper class, arrogant and exclusive. The Aunts' bearing was regal, their language was that of the Authorised Version which was their only reading. I cannot speak for my father because he died when I was six. From what I remember of his presence I exonerate him from all littleness, but the Aunts were snobs. Never were female 'companions' worse treated than Aunt Emily's Miss Millington. She might stand for the most miserable unliberated woman of the period. She was at fifty so outcast, so deprived of self-respect, so hopelessly trodden on as to have become in fact an object of contempt.

In all the houses of our relations there were aged retainers, butlers and nurses, excellent devoted servants who were worked unsparingly and, though respected, ignored. Perhaps sometimes they got a word of recognition, but I never heard it from my elders. I presume these old people stayed because they had nowhere else to go. Old age pensions did not exist and in any case they were, in this feudal way, part of the family. Yet they served with pride and the way my uncle's butler opened the door to me as a small girl, with a courtesy and a welcome greater than I got from my relations, stands out as one of my childhood's great pleasures.

The household served by this butler was wealthy. Uncle Holden, parent of our future guardian, lived in style. He was a big, fat man who spoke broad Yorkshire. His bearded kisses always smelled of soup. His beard was very long and as soft as a girl's hair. His eccentricities were our joy. He was deaf, and in order to save himself the trouble of holding his hand behind his ear he had caused to be made for himself a pair of tortoise-shell ears almost big enough for an African elephant, held in place by a spring fitting over the top of his head. These he wore in Chapel with great effect, and they enabled him to shout 'Alleluia' or 'Praise be to God' at suitable (to his idea) moments in the sermon. His wife, having the same doctor as all her sisters, had adopted delicacy. A whole service was too much for her, so just before the sermon Uncle in his grey frockcoat rose and left his pew to meet her alighting from her brougham at the door, and brought her in on his arm with imposing gallantry. This gave style to the service, and as our pew was level with theirs we had a good view of the little drama. Immediately in front of Uncle was an elderly lady who by some accident had her head permanently stuck sideways. To me it always made her hats look funny, as if she put the hat on to face forward though she could not. The fact that she was always in profile to Uncle made her the ideal informant when, in spite of his ears, he did not get the number of the hymn. He had only to tap her elbow and with an easy half turn of her waist she and Uncle were face to face and she could point with a gloved finger to her hymn book. This she did with a peculiarly graceful and sanctimonious half bow that was the delight of the six young Woods. At the end of the service Aunt was supported on her elephantine husband's arm down the aisle to the door, and generally one of us was taken in the brougham back to lunch. The house was spacious and imposing, handsomely furnished and worldly instead of cranky like ours. The food also was like nothing we ever saw or tasted at home. Uncle was a glutton. My sharp nursery eyes must have widened when the butler carried in two large plum puddings, one of which served five people and the other was lifted whole on to Uncle's plate. After lunch he slept and snored with a large handkerchief over his face. We were given toys—not Sunday ones—and told to play quietly. The favourite was something that may have been called a mobiloscope. It consisted of a circular cardboard container like a hat-box without a lid. It spun on a pedestal and its walls were perforated by high narrow slits every two inches. You fitted inside it long strips of what we should now call 'stills' of acrobats or steeple-chasers, spun the thing round and looked through the slits. Wonderful! The acrobats somersaulted, the cyclists cycled, the horses leapt. This was many years before the invention of the cinema.

It was a liberal house. Even the family portraits could be looked at with long pleasure. Uncle before he aged into gluttony and sleep must have been a lively generous fellow.

*

To return to our own other-worldly home, Mother was loved by her servants. She was not more generous to them than anybody else—a Christmas present would be an apron—but she was human and helped them in their family troubles. We had a laundry woman to whom I was much attached. I think of her whenever I see a Tintoretto goddess or nymph. She had an Italian type of face, the most beautiful rounded arms and a very soft voice. Her realm, reached down a black hole of winding, underground stairs, consisted of two vast cellars, one for the copper, the wash tub and dolly. Imagine a small wooden stool, or dolly, with four stout legs. Through the seat is set a three foot pole with a cross bar at the top. The stool fits easily into a high tub full of sheets whose folds wrap round the legs of the dolly. It must then be swished about as one holds the cross bar, the weight of the wet linen being quadrupled by the length of the pole. No one who has never used a dolly could guess what cruel work it is. The wash cellar was dark and always awash. It was underneath the eccentric drawing room, but no one there ever thought of it. The ironing cellar was a long tunnel underneath the dining room. It was festooned with clothes lines to take the sheets for twelve people. Rows of flat irons were ranged on the three sloping sides of the stove and a long table stood under the window where a grownup's eyes were on a level with the soil of the back garden. At the far end to which daylight never really reached were racks containing mysterious bales of things once belonging to my father or his father. It was believed by us all that among them was a mummy's hand. From these old bundles came a musty smell that seemed to confirm that belief. However one had only to get in among the hanging sheets for the mummy to be forgotten in the smell of Sunlight soap and dripping linen. Here Mrs Brade toiled alone all the year round. I used to go down, braving the dark stairs and the mummy hand, to have her sweet and gentle company and to iron doll's clothes. Once she surprised me by saying, 'Oh, Miss Lucy! To be here is my idea of Paradise!' I learnt later that she had a drunken husband who beat her frequently and that as a result, though she had had five longed-for babies, they had all been stillborn. When my mother died and the house was closed, she was the most heartbroken mourner.

*

Our three maid servants shared a large bedroom. They had no bath, but a wash basin and three large conspicuous chamber pots. The nursery suite had only a child-sized bath like a deep porcelain sink. Into this Frank and Phil and I were dumped together to scrub each other's backs pretending we were scrubbing floors. Nurse slept in the night nursery with Phil and me. No bath was provided for her.

Grandfather, the sea-bathing physician, had refused to consider allowing anything so dangerous as a boiler to be installed in his house. I was never intimate enough with my aunts to know if they had a bathroom or not. Father's, however, was the latest and most expensive that could be had. The bath was constructed like an enormous mahogany cradle of which the hood touched the ceiling. The inside of the hood was semicircular, finely perforated all round to give the 'Needle Spray'. At liver height there was a bruising 'Douche' and from the roof came two kinds of shower, normal or fierce. There was a control panel with many

My mother and father

My father

Lucy

Nurse

wheel-shaped knobs with their function printed on them and a dial with arrows to show how much hot to cold had been turned on. A mahogany lavatory seat as commodious as an armchair adjoined the bath, but its plumbing, alas, was primitive, being the same in principle as in British Rail today.

*

Mother's father was a Wesleyan minister who commanded love and respect, especially for his charity. I was told he was the bastard son of a West Country lord by a laundry maid. Apparently the bastardy outweighed the holiness and Mother was received into the family with a coldness amounting to cruelty, from all but one, Aunt Bertie, of whom I never heard as a child. She was never mentioned except once absent-mindedly by Mother, who named her as one of a group and said she had been very fond of her. Much later on her death bed, in her delirium she constantly called for Bertie. I remember her laughing with Father, but after his death I cannot remember her laughing again. It was not a love match—she married under pressure from her parents (they had seven daughters) when her inclination was elsewhere, to a man twice her age. Father had had a great love in youth for a wild-spirited girl who was killed in a hunting accident. Mother slightly resembled her in type of feature and was asked for as soon as seen. She was not like the horsewoman in character, but delicate, intensely sensitive and idealistic and without a trace of sensuous feeling. She bore, as Victorian wives had to, a child every year, but had little maternal feeling. Before she died she told me she wished she had never had any of us. She should have been a nun. She was very gentle. During my father's lifetime she was nearly always Mayoress. She must have had a civic life of which we knew nothing. She may have been very bad at it. Much entertaining of that kind can hardly have gone on without some echo of it reaching the nursery. My mother was not made for that kind of thing, and her idea of food was that it was a sad

(25)

necessity. Later on she began to think it was not even necessary and the boys raged with hunger.

It is extraordinary to me how little I remember of my father whose favourite I am told I was. Of his appearance I have no visual memory at all. I might have been blind. I remember the feel of his hand, his voice and laugh, and a comfortable confidence. He occasionally took us bathing in the shallow waveless sea that crawled across the sands to the Southport pier. He and we all wore the horizontally striped costumes that were the standard bathing outfit for men and children of the period. I imagine they were designed for decency, the stripes serving to cut up and conceal the shape of the wearer and produce hideousness. They are as I write high daytime fashion for the under thirties with whom hideousness is a cult.

There were holidays when Father was present. When the family travelled by train we had a reserved saloon and the station master met us at the station entrance, saw us bestowed, and waited to see us off. I remember him as wearing frock coat and top hat if only for such occasions. At any rate he was in full grandeur. The trains of course were those wonderful and never to be forgotten puff-puffs, the fury of whose puffs in the station threatened to burst my infant eardrums.

We stayed at Shap Wells hotel, now I believe submerged in a new reservoir. I walked with Father beside a stream and was shown by him how to throw leaves in the current for boats and run to follow them with joy and wonder. That puts me at about three years old. We walked through herds of Highland cattle, terrifying to me, but I was soothed by talk of God's providence—the soil for the worm, worm for the bird, bird for the table, and in face of these piercing-horned monsters my reaction should be, 'We thank Thee Lord for this our food'. Father was an obsessive preacher and I suppose he was good at it with his Biblical language and true passion. There was a settlement of miners on Shap Fell to whom he

preached! He had an idea that his little pigeon might be a
catcher of rough souls. He took me often between his knees
and taught me to sing,

> 'Will you meet me at the Fountain
> At the Fountain bright and fair?
> Will you meet me at the Fountain?
> Yes, I'll meet you, meet you there.'

When I had learnt it he told me he would take me with him
to the camp and I should sing to the miners. This never took
place. Probably my mother vetoed it.

*

Back in Southport he once took me with him to the Town
Hall and the Police Station. Hanging onto his hand I approved
the saluting and respect with which he was received, and his
authority. He said he would inspect the cells, and I should go
with him. Did he mean me to be impressed by the fate of
evildoers, especially of those who drank beer (he was a
teetotaller)? I only remember being held up to the spy
window in each door and seeing inside simply one of the
unhappy Poor, each crouching alone in a blank cell. I was
embarrassed. I still think it was inhuman to make a peepshow of them. Possibly the intention was not only that my
inexperienced soul should receive a lesson, but that the hard
hearts of the sinners within might be led to repentance by the
face of innocence. But my father was big-minded and warm-
hearted and I make him sound mean.

Once, when in some forgotten nursery squabble I had
bitten Phil's finger, I was marched downstairs by Nurse to
the dining room where Mother and Father were at table.
Their meal was interrupted while my heinous offence was
told, Nurse standing beside me like an indignant constable.
I pleaded in my own defence that I was just happening to
close my mouth when Phil put his finger in it. Father let out a
gale of laughter and I was dismissed with my sin and sub-
sequent lie unpunished.

(27)

That is absolutely all I can remember of my father, yet the thought of him always brings reverence and love.

*

Sometimes Nurse took us all in the horse-drawn tram to visit the Churchtown Botanic Gardens, a place offering a variety of strong emotions. The particular attraction was The Swings. It seems now a long way to go for such a simple pleasure, but they were imposing swings, hung from a height on iron-linked chains that my hands could just close round. I can still feel and hear them. One could swing sky-high whence the return was dreadful and always made me sick. The others would be there for hours, but I was taken by Nurse to find other interests. As one entered the big gates of the Gardens, there was the Museum, approached up a flight of steps guarded at the base by two stone lions crouching and gnashing. I would not have dared to come near them but for my upbringing on *Pilgrim's Progress*. Perhaps like the lions Christian had to pass they were really chained. Sustained by faith I bolted up the steps.

The Museum was full of terrors. First there were two human skeletons hanging side by side, male and female, horribly mobile. These pursued me home and through the night. Beside them was a dead tree wound around by a gigantic stuffed snake, sinister but by comparison bearable. It was only Garden of Eden stuff. There were rooms full of exhibits that have left no impression at all, but the worst things of all were what we called the waxworks. These were two glass-fronted boxes containing rigid doll's house figures. If one put a penny in the slot a nerve-awaking whirring began and things which should not move did so. One box was otherwise pleasing, showing merely bellringers in a tower who pulled on ropes while bells rang. The other was an execution scene ending with the gallows drop. But the subject was irrelevant. It was the age old terror of the inanimate moved by unseen power. It rivalled the martyr's stake as my nightmare for many years, chiefly in the imagination of the wide

(28)

Museum staircase at the bend of which sat a life-sized wax-work of a man, impudent and tense. All he did was, as one rounded the bend, to turn his head with a mechanical jerk to watch one pass. This was total horror. Emerging shaken from the Museum to rejoin the swingers, holding Nurse's hand I came up to a round bed completely filled with scented, velvety yellow pansies. This was the other side of the medal, a surprised joy that made an impression as deep. I have tried all my life to raise a bed as good, but that young rapture cannot be remade.

*

As we grew older attendants multiplied. Nurse had an underling, young and lively. Frances and Frank, the two immediately older than I, had an apple-cheeked Yorkshire girl, Eliza, whom we all loved. She came from Whitby and once to my great envy took Jamie and Frank home with her for a long visit. Picture postcards of high seas on that coast so impressed me that for years I collected photos of fountaining surf, though I had never seen or heard it.

On the floor below Eliza's charges was a governess for the two eldest, a Miss Shrewsbury, who had only one dress, of fudge-coloured serge from throat to floor. She never expected or found anything to smile about. Remembering her I sympathise with all the young ladies in Georgette Heyer's novels who fear governess-ship as the final horror, and exhausting and humiliating as Ivy Compton-Burnett shows it, my memory of it in reality is worse.

*

When I was six Father contracted pneumonia, almost a certain killer in the days before antibiotics. During his last days the setts of the whole street were covered deep in sand to deaden the noise of passing horse-drawn vehicles, but visitors came to inquire in a perpetual stream. A bulletin was hung outside the front door. These dramatic signs could be watched from the nursery window. I was as yet innocent of death and had no apprehension. About a year later a tame parrot died before my eyes and the realisation came with full force, but when before my father's funeral I was taken by Nurse and lifted up to put a lily of the valley in the cold hand, the weirdly dressed up doll lying in a box lined with pleated white satin did not draw a tear. We had never been allowed to visit him during his illness and what I now saw was meaningless; simply displeasing. Phil and I, too young to go to the funeral, were dressed in black and watched from our high windows the long cortege of hearse and carriages. Relatives in streaming black crêpe were handed into their broughams by gentlemen, top hat in hand, all in heavy but orderly silence, each vehicle moving away in turn with the creak of tautened harness and moving wheels. When all the chief mourners and civic representatives had gone, they were followed on foot by more people than I had thought existed. My filial pride swelled and I said to Nurse, 'Now I can never be happy again'. But as I said it I knew I was putting it on, and felt at that moment my first real personal shame. I feel sure that the evangelical teaching I had received had never got down to details such as 'Thou shalt not assume appropriate feelings'. Quite the opposite. I have seen one of my infant letters among my mother's treasures after she died. The baby writing obviously guided by an adult hand read, 'Little Lucy loves Mother but little Lucy loves Jesus more'. It is enough to make any adult blush, but I give myself credit for having an innate ethic that disclosed itself sternly at the age of six.

From this time on, as one elderly relative after another died, we were permanently dressed in black, mourning a year for each aunt or uncle deceased. By the time we were in our teens funerals had become an outrageous family charade. I did not get out of black till I was fifteen and Mother was in black all her life. I used to watch her dress for Chapel and groan at the ugliness of everything she put on.

After Father's death our life lost all magnitude. Each child had been left a small fortune to be spent on education during minority, but Mother in the mean Victorian fashion had only just enough to keep the house together and had she remarried would have forfeited all. She had no dynamism, no practical competence, and she had till now never made out a cheque. She was saved by having no interest in anything money could buy, a natural and extreme frugality and austerity. There were many negatives to her character, but if one awards a negative to each of the deadly sins and adds to that list no vulgarity, no inquisitiveness and no possessiveness, something grand remains.

I do not know how she bore her widowhood because about this time I fell ill and was sent to the Fever Hospital. It was thought to be a case of simultaneous measles and scarlet fever, the latter then a very dangerous disease. The hospital as I remember it was two corrugated iron wards at right angles to each other. At the end of my ward were two 'grownups', probably teenagers, too far away to know, and at the other myself. The nurses made a fuss of me and I enjoyed being there, except for a waggish nurse who scissored at me and said 'I will cut off your nose'. I believed her. It is curious that though obviously very ill I have no memory at all of feeling it. Perhaps children don't recognise a state that is not yet in their field of reference. When I was able to stand I was taken to the window from which one could see the men's ward at right angles. In their window another nurse supported a desperately white and ill one-legged boy, perhaps seven years old, with the face of an angel. I was told to wave to him and got a wan smile in return. That is the whole of my first love affair. Afterwards I was sent home and saw many doctors and was kept in bed in the dark for a time and was not allowed to walk for months. While I was in bed someone brought me a bunch of wallflowers whose velvet and scent was a joyful experience repeated every few minutes. So flowerless was my early childhood that I keenly remember each flower that I met. I also had, sent up from the kitchen to amuse me, a large potato with five knobs (head and four legs) which to me was as an adored puppy. There came a day when

Nurse relentlessly removed both flowers and puppy saying they were going bad. I wept for a cruel bereavement and was told 'not to behave silly'. She did not think as she whisked them away that at eighty-five I would still feel it. During my convalescence I was given *Alice in Wonderland*, the first non-pi book, a fascinating delight. I was still dependent on being read to and fought petulant battles with Nurse to make her read it when she was busy. 'What do you want that stupid book for?'

*

We had been left, as was usual for fatherless children, to the guardianship of a cousin on the Wood side, a very capable man of perhaps thirty years old. He evidently took his responsibilities seriously, perhaps a little too much so, coming as he did in my mother's mind from the enemy side of the family. She flared up and told him to leave her children to her. Nevertheless he was entirely good and generous, never let us see there had been any difficulty and was tolerant, loving and helpful always. From the time when I sat on his knee and blew to make his Hunter watch spring open and chime, I was as devoted to him as if he had been a much older brother. His total integrity and courtesy were an education of the kind that is so profound as to be taken for granted.

In Mother's now reduced circumstances the governesses and undernurses vanished. Nurse was left, as her faithful help, and we all went to school. The boys' and ours were in adjacent streets. The two eldest boys went to 'Miss Clough's'. She was probably a Wesleyan because from their talk their education was more 'pi' than ours. (Jamie at ten became an enthusiastic temperance canvasser and drew us all into it.) We all set off together every morning, at first by horse tram but later on foot, a walk of about two miles through the town. We passed every day the same gentlemen walking briskly in the opposite direction to their offices. Cars were not yet known. If you were not grand enough to keep a groom and brougham, you walked. These gentlemen all had nicknames.

One dapper little man always had his pockets full of chocolates for us. These morning walks through silent residential streets were enjoyable, especially in spring when every front garden had overhanging hawthorn trees in bloom.

My youngest brother Phil had curly hair as fine as cobweb and the colour of polished brass. It came down nearly to his waist and was considered too beautiful to be cut off. The poor little Samson was sent at six with me to a private school of about forty girls. It was run by a severe, immaculately gowned woman with glossy hair smoothed back from a marble brow. She was helped by her monstrous mother, heavily bombazined and with a lace cap over her white hair. There were also two pupil teachers, really schoolgirls with their hair up.

My first morning began with writing the alphabet on a slate. In the lowest class all the work was done on slates, lovable objects, the pleasant drag of the pencil making a soft sound and leaving a beautiful line. I could already read and write, but poor Phil, screened and embarrassed by his trailing cloud of hair, did not succeed in either until he was ten, though as intelligent as any. Even at home he hardly ever spoke, so that the three or four sentences he is known to have uttered were never forgotten. We were all astounded to learn from the report of his last year at a public school, that he was a brilliant debater. I wish I had known the brother that strangers knew.

The second lesson of the first day at school was reading. The passage beginners were given was not 'The cat sat on the mat' which had explained reading to me in a couple of glances at home, but we plunged straight into the deep end of literature.

'Remember now thy Creator in the days of thy youth while the evil days come not, nor the years draw nigh when thou shalt say, I have no pleasure in them; while the sun, or the light, or the moon, or the stars, be not darkened, nor the clouds return after the rain; in the day when the keepers of

the house shall tremble, and the strong men shall bow themselves, and the grinders cease because they are few, and those
that look out of the windows be darkened, and the doors shall
be shut in the streets, when the sound of the grinding is low,
and he shall rise up at the voice of the bird, and all the daughters
of musick shall be brought low; also when they shall be afraid
of that which is high, and fears shall be in the way, and the
almond tree shall flourish, and the grasshopper shall be a
burden, and desire shall fail; because man goeth to his long
home, and the mourners go about the streets; or ever the
silver cord be loosed, or the golden bowl be broken, or the
pitcher be broken at the fountain, or the wheel broken at the
cistern. Then shall the dust return to the earth as it was: and
the spirit shall return unto God who gave it.'

This was stuttered and stammered over round the class with
reluctance. I had of course heard it before, but it seemed to
me now a revelation and a glory in words. I do not think anyone except perhaps my father would give that passage to a
seven-year-old expecting it to be greedily received as what
reading had to offer. When I see modern reading primers I am
aghast at their mean vulgarity. In my day I guess this passage
was a moral gesture for the beginning of term. We went on
from it to *Coral Island*, and afterwards when we got to
'Literature' we were given the facile jungle of Scott. But on
that first day I had taken hold of the real thing.

The grim bombazine dowager, ruler in hand for the rapping
of knuckles, taught me to play scales, but for singing we had
the choirmaster of the biggest church in the town. (He
appears in *The Children of Green Knowe* as the choirmaster of
Great Church.) There was no piano in the big classroom but
he brought a tuning fork and a linen roller that he hung on
the wall, printed with Doh Re Mi etc. As he pointed to each
word we had to sing the notes. Squatting on the floor in the
front row among the youngest I joined in with the others and
sang what they sang. I had no idea what it was all about. We
also learned songs, such as 'The Minstrel Boy' and 'She is far

from the land' (where her young lover sleeps). It was while we were learning the latter that the master, holding up the class, pointed his cane at me and told me to sing it alone. I was gratified and piped up to my maximum noise, probably about that of a new-born kitten. He turned away putting his hand over his mouth, having enjoyed his little joke without unkindness.

In those early schooldays I made no friends. There were only two Wesleyans in the school. One was the friend of my sister Frances. They would not allow me to walk with them to school. I had to follow behind. The other I was told by my mother not to speak to 'because she was vulgar'. Otherwise I do not remember the face and name of a single child in my first years. Probably we were oddities and tended to get left out. We never went into any of their homes nor had them to ours. The text we were brought up on was 'Come out of her, my children, (Babylon, the Great Whore) *and be ye different*'. The only party I remember from that time was in the house of a cousin of my parents' generation. I had not been there before and was shy and frightened as Nurse dressed me in unlikely party clothes.

We had no carriage. The only form of transport was the horse-cab. There was a cab rank at the end of our street where the cabbies had a shelter provided by my father. The cabbies and their drooping horses were a familiar feature of our life. The cabs were old, rickety and smelly. The smell was extraordinary. I always presumed that somehow both horse and driver slept inside. The feel of the dusty upholstery under one's fingers was repulsive. There was a current legend that once when one of the Aunts was being driven, the bottom had fallen out of the cab, forcing her in her long skirts and elastic-sided boots to run along inside keeping up with the horse. Which would not be difficult. The silliest of our middle-aged cousins, who at fifty had a face like a highly coloured Dutch doll, wore forget-me-nots in her hair and cooed like a woodpigeon. She ran a mission for cabmen. I don't know what she offered them. My brother Frank added to the standard bedside prayer which was 'God Bless' (all our relations in order) 'And bless the cab horses and keep them warm tonight'.

To return to my first party, it was a large and overpowering party. I sat at the long table beside an unknown, mischievous not to say malicious-looking boy a year older than myself. He made one remark, pointing to an elderly man at the head of the table, 'You see that man over there holding up his knife? If you don't behave he'll roar at you and have you sent out.' Had I known it, this was his father and my host. I ate in misery and silence. Twenty years later I married that boy, malice and all.

*

The teaching in school was very simple: for arithmetic we learned the multiplication tables and weights and measures. For history we learned by heart the dates of all the kings and queens of England, one dynasty a week. For literature we learned a simple poem such as Wordsworth's 'Daffodils'. Learning by heart, even when, like the mere names of kings, it was meaningless, I found quite as much fun as, say, Ludo or Snap. It was something to do. But the bulk of the class seemed simply to sit through every lesson without the slightest interest or effort. Simple (if idiotic) questions such as 'And what happened to Wordsworth as he lay on his couch?' went round the class and found no answer. No one seemed to mind, neither pupil nor teacher—who expected it. This attitude continued right through the school. None of these girls was going to earn her own living. There was no pressure at all, no Eleven plus, no O or A level. They saw no point in learning. They were there to be kept out of mischief till they grew up. Three years of this uneventful life have left no vivid memory but the sickly scent of privet in the school playground and the way a pretty pupil teacher did her hair.

*

At home we now saw more of our mother. Relieved from her

Mayoral duties she turned to us. She had also acquired a friend, the only one she ever had, but she was one in a thousand, and being single spent most of her time with us. Her name was Patty Ashton. In appearance she was as like a pullet as a human being can possibly be, though her eyes were blue in a wattle-pink face. She was therefore very funny to look at, and spinsterish to the last feather. One of the family jokes was her woollen combinations, seen on the clothes line, long-sleeved and long-legged *and* with a knee-length skirt added for decency. The trade name was Modesta. She claimed to have only five of the seven layers of skin, and it may well have been true, she was so available. She was the most loving and understanding person I have known, in all family acerbities equally sympathetic with all, with a merry sense of humour that had no edge. I took all my bruises and fears to her and was always comforted. None of us took her seriously, but she was my mother's sole support throughout their lives and her comic goodness gentled everything.

*

If my father's religion was personal and passionate, my mother's beliefs were 'received' and were as certain as tenets never questioned. Every word of Scripture was literally true, including the creation of the world in six days. But to the ten commandments she added four more:

> Thou shalt not drink alcohol;
> Thou shalt not go to the theatre;
> Thou shalt not play cards;
> Thou shalt not dance.

These were held as stringently as those given to Moses. She was also anti-Catholic without any qualification, as were my aunts, one of whom was heard to tell her companion to draw the curtains as two nuns walked past in the street, so that 'those *devilish snakes*' should neither see nor be seen. In Foxe's *Book of Martyrs* the martyrs are all Protestant and we as children were taught that the stake was a likely fate for us.

(37)

'The fires of Smithfield will be relit.' I do not know how much the rest of the family was affected—none of them ever said anything to me that reflected my fears—but night after night in my dreams I recanted at the stake, I only, all the others being burned—off stage, I am glad to say. My imagination was not equal to witnessing it. I always woke terrified and totally ashamed. During some domestic shift or other I shared a bedroom with my brother Frank, to whom I confessed that I was afraid to go to sleep because of my dreams. He rose tenderly to the occasion and with talk and riddles kept me awake as long as we both could hold out. So great was my terror of burning that it made me shake even to burn a piece of paper. Fire phobia pursued me into my thirties. During Hitler's time when hideous martyrdoms were a daily occurrence I wondered whether I ought to be grateful for such an unflinching upbringing which was after all not out of date but very actual. Yet I doubt if terror in childhood is a help if the moment comes. I was practised in recanting.

Another night pastime Frank and I shared was to stand side by side behind the bedroom curtains to watch the windows of the houses opposite. They were separated from us by our back garden, the lane for the back gate, and their back gardens. The occupants must have thought that with so much space and two high walls between, they were not overlooked. A whole street of back windows was lit up for us to watch. On the ground floor were the kitchens, on the first floor several dentists' surgeries where nothing was going on, and above that bedrooms. We never saw anything traumatic or even dramatic, but it was a fascinating peepshow. Even the passing up and down stairs, the private conversations snatched in empty rooms, the order given and obeyed at a run, were sufficiently mysterious and the whole thing toy-like and pretty in the surrounding dark.

*

From the fourteen commandments the forbidding of music was by some oversight omitted, probably because, except for hymns, it had not been heard of in my mother's family. I can't believe my father was indifferent. Not only was he distantly part Jewish, but in our generation music broke out all round. However, all I have to put to his credit musically was a collection of delightful musical boxes, beautifully veneered and decorated, playing Scotch airs in a very sweet tone. There was also a large square box on legs. Into it one put discs the size of a modern record covered all over with sharp wire bristles. It gave out a displeasing sound like a harmonium. Quite recently there was a talk about these on the radio, and I heard the old queezy sound again.

2

A great change came when, for Mother's health, we all moved
into Westmorland for a year. We lodged in a large house
beside the river Kent at Arnside and my real life began,
at ten years old. The village was small enough for us to
know every inhabitant, and in any case we were well
known because our maternal grandfather had lived there.
The steep little cliff path that led to his house was known
by his name, Garrett's path. My mother's unmarried sisters
still owned it.

The house where we were installed was kept by two sisters,
Annie whom we all loved and her cross elder, known to us as
Flop-legs. It was furnished much better than the usual
lodging house, with handsome, farmhouse mahogany and
beautiful china. There were big oil paintings of horses
ploughing or returning at dusk which I much preferred to our
ancestors at home. They must have had some merit for I
looked at them constantly, never disappointed. The sisters
must have come down in the world a long way. We occupied
the house not only for that year but for many summers
afterwards. It was a second home. It stood on what was called
The Promenade, a macadamed cul-de-sac fronting eight or
ten houses. It was wide enough for a char-à-banc to turn
round and was edged with a sea wall along the river. From
our windows we looked across the wide estuary of wet sand to
Grange on the far side with Cartmel Fell behind. Upstream
we saw the real fells, blue or sandy-coloured against the sky.
What brings all this and the sharp smell most vividly and

nostalgically alive is the sound of swifts, who built under the eaves and screamed and looped for ever in a weaving host round the bedroom windows.

The estuary of the river Kent was glorified twice daily with the drama of the 'bore', the tidal wave. All my days pivoted upon the time of its expected arrival, the waiting stillness of the shining expanse in which only a small shallow channel of the river remained, hardly enough to float a rowing boat; the expectant cries of the gulls forestalling what must be, and at last at an incredible speed the heaped up waters of the Irish Sea poured in, headed by a low but tearing wave churning and eating the sand as it went till in no time there was deep water, a mile wide with a dangerous undulating force along the centre, making for the viaduct where it eddied in tumult among the piers. The viaduct at that time was entirely wooden. The small steam-powered trains crossing it made a most musical muffled thunder, louder when the tide was out, but always delightful. Later on it was rebuilt in iron and lost all its magic.

We quickly knew all the boatmen, and were welcomed in the boat sheds where small yachts were made. All the boats on this stretch of the river were locally made and we knew them all by name. The boatmen were very tolerant of us, perhaps for our grandfather's sake. They taught us the risks of the bore and how to deal with it, and at what distance it was safe to follow it in a boat, and even how one might meet it head on, but that was for Jamie only. They allowed Frank and me, with our thin childish arms, to row about as much as we liked. When not in a real boat, a toy one, stripped of its mast which always toppled it over, was my Argos, drawn by a string round dangerous reefs, in and out of tiny bays along the bank. The imaginative pleasure I got from this over-spilled into pure happiness, blue sky, gulls' cries, vast distances and wet sand between my toes. It strikes me now as interesting that a small child can at the same age play with a risky tidal wave than which nothing could be more objective, and draw a chip of wood by a thread, feeling that to be the more complete experience.

The valley is closed in by hills and fells rising behind them, whose outlines were my constant reference and grounds for confidence. The river, whose every mood, current, sandbank, curve, rock, cliff and cove I came to know intimately, was by far the biggest experience of my early life, an in-built way of thinking.

Besides the river there was the wooded hilly country all round, as yet completely natural and open to us in every direction as far as we could go, and we roamed far. There were no cars, no buses, nothing that we now would call a road, only larger or smaller lanes. We travelled on foot, but if we really wanted to reach a town, such as Kendal, we could cycle, sure of meeting nothing worse than a milk float or pony cart.

There were two schools in the village, both much better than those we were used to. The girls' school was a converted country house, very pretty and beautifully situated. There were teachers with whom it was a challenge to learn, whose discipline was admired and whose approval was a quick joy. There was only one classroom, smaller groups used the living rooms of the old house; no assembly hall, no gymnasium, and the hockey field was a lop-sided valley with a goal post at the top of each of its hills. Nobody thought this was a disadvantage. In this school I was happy every moment.

The boys also were content. Phil with his hair at last cut short could go with Frank and they were taught by real men, one of whom was an idol whose name was forever in their chatter. Jamie, hereafter referred to as Jas, was away at boarding school, Rydal Mount.

*

The eldest of us, Mary, was the physical scapegoat of the family. She embodied all weaknesses and diseases and the rest of us were totally healthy—she was plain and her figure was almost deformed, but she had elegant hands and feet.

She was at sixteen intelligent, dignified and able. Under other circumstances she could have done much, but her handicaps were so great that nothing else could ever happen to her. She was lonely and reserved, but amiable with the younger ones. Jas was the dominant male, demanding and receiving homage and admiration and imitation from all, but especially from me, for I adored him. Frances I saw little of. Though so near in age and almost identical in appearance, we had nothing in common. She had a mother fixation and was always hanging on to her skirts. Frank was self-effacing but my constant companion. Phil—handsome, silent but laughter provoking— was everyone's favourite. Patty Ashton and Nurse were there to support Mother.

*

I particularly remember the snowy winter of that year. We went to school in the morning and returned at night in the dark, carrying swinging lanterns that held a candle. There were as yet no electric torches. The way was up Garrett's path, a steep footpath up the edge of a rocky bluff. It was fenced on both sides and for some reason had a kissing gate every twenty yards or so. The falling snowflakes were caught by the candlelight as they danced past and if I swung my arm the golden circle met white wadded fencing on the left and then on the right, still there though constantly disappearing. When my feet told me we must by now be approaching a gate, the exploring light would find the friendly landmark magically transformed and kissed again and again by the flakes that came in from the surrounding blackness. Each gate told me exactly where in the obliterated universe I stood, in my little circle of candlelight. This treasured adventure was entirely private.

*

Now came my first spring in the country. Hitherto spring had only meant the double red or white hawthorns along the town streets. The idea of a front garden as status symbol had not come in. I do not remember seeing a daffodil even in the park, the soil of Southport was so deadly poor. I cannot remember when I first smelled lilac though the thought dilates my nostrils and in memory fingers still small enough to match the single florets hold them in wonder. These tiny experiences have the size of revelation. The world opened wide, to let in what?

My mother, penny careful (she gave a tenth of her income to charity), never had a flower in the house. Now at Arnside I received the full impact of the returning sun. Every inch of that earth responded. There were fields of wild daffodils, those slender little flowers with white haloes and primrose trumpets, infinitely more beautiful than the dandelion-coloured giants of today. For sixpence the farmer would let us pick till we were tired and could not hold any more. In the open country and across the commons primroses and violets were everywhere while the smell of the earth itself was intoxicating. The scent of a bunch of primroses must be one of the sweetest things in childhood. Walking across the 'near common' on springing turf kept smooth as a lawn by rabbits, we came to Newbarns Bay, a big scoop of wet, grey sand only covered at high tide and smelling violently of river. There was a farm here providing delicious home-made meals served by a severely reserved fifteen-year-old lass who was Jas's first infatuation. Here too there were woods carpeted with lilies of the valley and wood anemones.

Beyond Newbarns came the 'far common', larger and still more beautiful. The footpath across it was little more than a rabbit track, hardly visible. I do not remember ever meeting anyone else on it, and litter was not yet invented. It led ultimately through a limestone stile to another bay called White-grate, surrounded by a limestone rock face ten or twelve feet high. Unlike Newbarns this cove was floored with a shelving bank of white limestone pebbles which occurred nowhere else that I know of in the course of the river. They not only gave off a rainbow light that surprised the eye, but also a clean chalky smell. This was a favourite picnic place, magical to the senses. From here one looked more down the estuary than across it—an immense area of sandbank, and wandering channels, growing ever wider toward the imagined horizon and reputed to have stretches of deadly quicksands.

Above the miniature cliffs a track ran through an oak coppice, scarlet-leaved because rooted in limestone, giving off an exciting aroma. Primroses rioted in the oak roots. The path was overgrown and hardly passable for an adult but it was then and for twenty years afterwards my particular and secret kingdom. It led ultimately through a deserted village, (abandoned perhaps in the Black Death?), a cluster of half a dozen ruined cottages, built of stone but now hardly higher than a ground plan, overgrown with brambles and nettles, ferns rooting in what was once a window sill, a room full of tangled growth and a butterfly passing through. I haunted it. How could desolation have happened in what seemed to me the most perfect place in which one could ever live?

*

I have taken the reader a long walk with my ten-year-old self round the base of a hill called the Knot, having the estuary on our right hand all the way. After the Deserted Village one came scrambling down to another bay and then the path turned inland to a wide, green valley in which stood Arnside Tower, a square ruined Peel tower such as were dotted about the district. The romance of the great desolate walls with windows to non-existent rooms and corner spiral stairways ending in space was the seed that burst into life when I found my present house.

From the Tower, a path led through the larch woods of the Knot, and finally down an undulating hillside clothed with bracken fronds of another unforgettable scent, back to the village. The impact of such rich, varied and vital experience on an imagination reared on sterile sand and Foxe's *Book of Martyrs* was explosive. Suddenly I was myself. What chance have children who grow up in a tower block and walk, if at all, in streets smelling of diesel, who have never heard a robin in his own woodland singing his happiness in that lively stillness?

*

The joys of Arnside were wide and inexhaustible. A long walk inland took us through oxlip woods and cornfields full of wild flowers (no weed killers yet!) to a farm where I was once permitted to see in his stall a bull as huge as a steam engine but with every inch of his hide charged with danger. He had an eye like a smouldering furnace and a head and neck heavy enough to demolish anything. He was tethered by his dribbling nostrils.

Beyond the farm was a hill covered with limestone, at the summit of which were the Fairy Steps, the object of our excursions. We went through a wood where the trees grew out of crevices between horizontal limestone strata. The crevices were full of ferns and mosses and of unguessed depth, very mysterious. The stone was a pale bluish silver, half polished, which gave a curious light to the wood. The Fairy Steps, small, regular and absolutely natural, wound up through a crack just wide enough for children to pass, almost impossible for buxom Nurse, on to a plateau. This was before the era of trippers and there was nothing to diminish the magic. Only a rabbit track led to the steps and all about on the turf sprawled lichen-covered boulders that to my finger were clearly alive. Sitting up there on one of those warm stones that felt akin to me, as it were ancestral, the view comprised everything that I knew and loved, bounded by the familiar outline of the distant fells. This acknowledgment superimposed again and again, accumulating depths of recognition, cannot be traced back to a first time, but it works there, the basis of all that came after.

*

More accurately placed in time are the pleasures of the Three Springs. Out of the tree-crowned bank of the river there gushed, overflowing a stone trough, a stream that ran down the sand. Here in the holidays all the little Woods busily

made a series of dams to hold up the stream, one basin below
the other, with turf gates to control the flow. To be spade in
hand became second nature—and still is. Often now when
amateur gardeners offer their help and I give them a spade, I
see instantly that they have never used one. They have no
idea how to handle what to me is as simple as walking. With
so obvious a tool it is still possible to do everything awkwardly
and inefficiently. Then I remember the Three Springs, the
first wooden spade thrown away as silly, the tin blade which
bent backwards if you asked too much of it. But as we were
always barefoot, the final satisfaction of the slam of the boot
must have come later.

*

Summer brought another range of flowers whose names my
mother taught me. The grass of the hillside was closely interlaced with rock roses in an endless spread, you could lie on
them in the sun, and 'I know a bank whereon the wild thyme
blows' became afterwards a passionate personal avowal. Here
I met harebells, a flower of such delicate under-statement
that it almost seems the most beautiful thing ever.

Autumn brought blackberrying, and the highest tides,
boats moored on the shore being dragged under water
because their anchor ropes were not equal to the depth and
the Irish Sea was awash over the small inland promenade.

*

This glorious year came to an end and we were back in
Southport. Every night in bed I wept in tearing grief for all I
was now parted from. I wanted instead of pavements the feel
under my feet of the worn rocks along the shore, of the sweet
turf of the hills where every gradient was a muscular pleasure.
I wanted the night sounds of the river life, flocks of sandpipers
in flight, curlews and solitary gulls. The promise of next year
was too remote to mean anything. For children NOW is
inescapable. Not to have that boundless joy NOW was
despair. I think I felt as much then as later on I felt for an
absent lover.

(47)

About this time also my brother Frank went to boarding school at Rydal Mount. Mother and I went with him to Colwyn Bay. He was upset and to my astonishment and pleasure held my hand in the train. I could hardly believe it. We had never been taught to kiss our brothers and sisters and had never done so. This was the only physical contact I ever had with any member of my family, bearded uncles excepted. Mother and I stayed the night at Colwyn Bay, and the next morning at the hour of the school break we went to see the poor boy in the playground where he stood alone by the fence. We gave him a bun, as sad as if we had left him in a zoo.

Frances and I went to the same school as before. She was going through a period of malicious teasing, of being aggravating for the sheer pleasure of it. We now shared a bedroom where there was bitter friction about nothing. Any little thing will serve a child to show spite, and it never fails to find its mark. However, Fortune now sent me a friend. A new girl came to the school who was unlike anyone I had met before. Connie was an Irish Catholic and came from a cultured family. She had long fair hair and magnificent blue eyes set in very full upper and lower lids. She might on account of her little animal nose have been called Piggy, had not her expression been both so proud and so voluptuous. She was as unathletic (hockey was our game) and as lithe as a young cat, with hands and feet almost as small. Even when adult she took size 2 in shoes. We paired up instantly. If we were the opposites of each other we were both unlike all the rest.

Connie's parents lived halfway between the school and our house. It was probably on the day of our first meeting that I went home with her. It was a house where everything pleased the eye and it had its own very pleasant smell. Her mother was elegantly simple and made me welcome with a sweet smile. Thereafter she never inquired what we did.

On that first day we went straight up to Connie's room. She had a wooden bedstead that I thought marked her out as one

Uncle Holden

Father with Frank and Lucy

of the élite. Ours were all push-bike iron. More surprising still, Connie had a bookcase by her bed. We had only one in the house, except in Father's closed up study, and few of what filled those shelves could be called books. They were sermons, treatises on engineering and papers. Mother's few classics were in the breakfast room—*Cranford*, Jane Austen, Dickens, Meredith. Connie had a wealth of books, including everything illustrated by Rackham or Dulac. Her whole room also was frilled and deliberately charming. Her mother couldn't go wrong.

Connie introduced me to the pleasure of blowing bubbles. She made this an outlet for her whole personality. When the trembling distended irridescence was loosed from the pipe and mounted like a balloon, she watched it with greater concentration, seeing more than anyone else could. Everything she did was filled to the brim with vitality and imagination.

Another feature of this household that was a revelation to me was the position of the servants. There were two, both very old, white-haired and frail. They had served the family through two generations and were treated with love and reverence as if they had been grandmothers. When they came into the room, they came smiling as friends, not as servants. I looked on at this and saw that it was good.

Connie had a passion for poetry. Our chief amusement together was learning by heart. If at school the class was asked to memorise (though that word was not then used) a famous passage from 'Marmion' or 'The Lady of the Lake', Connie and I would have privately learned half the book simply for pleasure. This we did on long walks together, often on the desolate marshy sands stretching between Southport and Lytham, which had a horizonless steamy beauty and the song of larks. We chanted 'The Ancient Mariner'. Connie, who was as morbid as she was sensuous, particularly loved 'the nightmare Life-in-Death . . . who thicks man's blood with cold', but my favourite lines were 'Softly she was going up, And a star or two beside'. Not very long ago I was working in

(49)

my garden when I heard a small boy high in an elm which overhung the river. He believed himself to be alone, and in his high clear voice, as loud and carrying as a thrush, he was chanting, as if hanging in the shrouds,

> 'The sun came up upon the left
> Out of the sea came he!
> And he shone bright, and on the right
> Went down into the sea.'

Verse after verse rang out, and I 'blessed him unaware'.

Connie also introduced me to Omar Khayyám, which my mother would certainly not have allowed, and that also we learned. It precipitated all those discussions about time and eternity that I suppose all twelve-year-olds thrash about in. She claimed to have abandoned all religious belief. Only one thing mattered—never to hurt anyone or anything. She was therefore a vegetarian and I became one. I remember to Mother's credit that she neither resented nor argued against this tiresomeness. She quietly let me get so hungry on apples and bananas that ultimately I gave way.

It was not only poetry I learned by heart, there is prose that anchors itself in the memory, pre-eminently the Authorised Version of the Bible, of which I could quote great parts without having intentionally learned it, notably Genesis, Job, the Song of Deborah, the Song of Solomon, the Gospels and the Book of Revelation. There was also *Pilgrim's Progress*. I knew *Alice in Wonderland* word by word, the Jungle Books, and of course *Uncle Remus*. Prose should be memorable. To go right down the age groups, *Little Black Sambo* (now it seems colour-barred) is a miracle of memorability, perfect prose.

I spent a great deal of time in Connie's house. There was nothing to attract her to mine and we omitted it without a thought. Her mother put me up in the great curtained bed of the spare room where Connie and I talked the whole night through. How do children find so much to talk about? It bubbled happily on non-stop.

It was a regular practice in those days to sleep two in a bed. Even the boarders at school shared double beds. But when I ultimately at sixteen got to a Quaker boarding school, though the Head mistress had not yet caught up with electric light, she had caught up with other notions in the air, and any girl found in bed with a friend was expelled. Nowadays all is different again.

*

My mother had only one fear, and that was sex. While we were too young for it she never questioned what we were doing and was very tolerant of our fads and enthusiasms and let them run their normal course. I doubt if she knew Connie by sight. Certainly she never opposed the friendship, perhaps because I was very much alone.

Frances was ill. She had the newly fashionable disease, appendicitis. It was decided she should have the operation— then large and serious—at home. The schoolroom was cleared, stripped of its wallpaper and disinfected, all while the patient waited, so the operation cannot have been urgent. Two trained nurses were brought in and Frances was operated upon on the schoolroom table. The operation, if it had ever been necessary, was presumably successful, but owing perhaps to the difficulties of surgery in a private house and the lack of routine, four hot bottles were placed against the patient's legs without covers and four serious deep burns resulted. The surgeon was for dismissing the nurses at once but Mother showed her essential goodness by refusing. Their careers would have been ruined, whereas it was certain they would never make this mistake again. They remained in the house a very long time as Frances was suffering from shock and in great pain. The dressing of her burns was agony twice daily. She was given a wooden penholder to bite on so that she would not scream. I watched with awe and reverence, as if she was bearing it in my place, as it were for me. I felt exactly the same sixty years later when she died with fortitude.

In fact, her health and nervous system never recovered and she became more than ever a 'mother's girl'.

*

While Connie was widening my horizons on one side, on the other my evangelical background was fighting its last battle. There was a yearly event called the Convention which was spoken of at home as of great importance. It may even have been held in memory of Father or financed in his will. In a field beside the Chapel a tent was erected as big as a circus Big Top. As far as I was concerned the tent was the Convention. It had a splendid looping shape and a strange subdued but lively light. The edge of the canopy where it met the upright walls was decorated with semicircular flaps that shifted and whispered and let in flying sunrays. Many tall masts leant this way or that supporting the roof. The whole thing creaked in the wind and took huge breaths. I so loved the tent that I went to meetings willingly and often during the week that the Convention lasted. It was run very much on Billy Graham lines, but without his organised showmanship. Emotional speakers pleaded with us to be saved and described their own experience of the bliss and certainty that followed. They implored us with every hysterical or hypnotic trick they could command to stand up if we were 'Saved'. Who should be saved if not I, brought up as I had been? I stood up. No feeling of bliss followed, only of doubtful embarrassment. Clearly I was not saved. I brooded over this for some days and returned to the fascinating tent to watch and listen to its secretive moving and breathing. The orators turned on the pressure again and I thought, I was not saved last time. I will be this time definitely and for certain. I stood up again and even went so far as to follow the other would-be saved to the foot of the platform, to be received and congratulated by the orators as new members of the heavenly club, or as tricks they had won. I went home even less confident than before, feeling that if this was all, at least I had done all I could. As I entered the house I heard my sister Mary burst into Mother's room

(52)

and say, 'Lucy's been saved again!' And Mother and Patty Ashton and Mary all laughed. Rooted to the stairs, I realised that all this about the Convention was hypocrisy. They encouraged me to go and really thought it was silly. From that moment all my mother's teaching was invalidated. Of course I was emptying out the baby with the bath water, but some hypocrisy there certainly was, also what at my present age I dislike even more, the snobbery of dealing out vulgar religion for 'the others'. The Convention was again nothing more than a flapping tent. To give credit where it is due, Mary never wasted words and her brief rebukes cured me of many things. 'It's silly to say Nobody loves me' stopped that silliness for ever, and when I talked too much she said, 'Don't be so ebullient'. I had no idea what the word meant but it was all the more efficacious for that. I ceased to be a babbler.

*

I must have been about twelve years old when our guardian married. The bride was a lady of wealth and great civic standing in Manchester. She was spoken of with awe and some apprehension. When he brought her to see us I was dumbfounded. She was an immense woman with ginger hair, to my young eyes ludicrously overdressed, over-hatted, over-veiled and scented, sweeping round like a tidal wave. She was much older than he and I couldn't understand it. However there he was, his eyes starry with pride and gratitude, running after her, carrying her voluminous wraps and parcels. Frances and I were to be bridesmaids and for this were dressed in rose pink silk in tiers of frills from neck to hem. To me, accustomed to the plainest black or white, this dress was admissible for a charade like a wedding but an agony of overdressing for later occasions. I had to go to school concerts dressed like a Christmas cracker. Fortunately the death of Beady Liz put me back in black.

Our new cousin-in-law took us on as part of her marital opportunities for organising. She invited me to tea. Her house was the best run establishment in the town, nothing in it but the most luxurious and modern. Her maids were trained and starched to perfection. I took in everything with interest and surprise. In spite of what seemed excessive splendour, it was both comfortable and effortless.

After tea my hostess got to work on me. She had decided that I was to be a medical missionary and outlined to me, as if it were a known certainty, what my education was to be, in order that I might go to Oxford or Cambridge or London. I wriggled in embarrassment, having no intention of being a missionary, but what can a young guest do when so overborne and overlooked, with a proud guardian watching his wife's dynamism so approvingly? I listened politely to all congratulations on my future and shuddered. Presently she sent her husband out of the room to fetch something, and then said to me, meaning I believe to flatter me with a suggestion of being all women together, perhaps a practised manoeuvre, 'I can't help laughing at him. He's like a little boy.'

My rage at this condescension to my loved guardian was so great that I was fortified for ever *not* to be a missionary.

*

There was a day when the first car appeared in Southport. Those who had seen it rushed home to say so, but this sign of the end of our world was less important to us than the new Helter-Skelter tower in the fun-fair on the sands. It was some time before I was actually taken for a drive. I found it far less pleasurable than the two-horse wagonette or char-à-banc in which we went for school excursions. If I was quick enough off the mark, I usually managed to get a seat on the box beside the driver where besides being high above the hedges with a good view of the country, I could enjoy the rolling rumps of the horses and the piston-like movement of their stifles, together with the rich smell of horse and leather, the jingle, the tossing and the musical clip clop. One could not of course cover great distances, but every minute of the progress could be taken in, caressed by the eyes, breathed in, smelled and remembered. We did not merely see things whizz by, we moved along as a natural part of the country, we arrived, as it were, all the time.

The motor car was not the only innovation. About this time Frank and I saw our first Moving Picture. The theatre was forbidden us because of the supposed immorality of actresses, but there was nothing about the camera to lead Mother to guess at the lives of future film stars. Indeed nothing could have been purer than our first film. It was called *Our Glorious Navy* and showed battleships putting out to sea in a technical hailstorm and sailors cheering. We came out happy that our navy was so glorious. This must have been a freak show put out for propaganda. It was in the Town Hall, there were not yet any cinemas. I do not remember going to a Moving Picture again until some years later when *Hamlet* was filmed, played by the ageing Forbes Robertson. It was shown in the local theatre and I was allowed across the guilty threshold to see it. I was so moved by the play that on the way home I walked slap into a lamp post, hurting myself considerably, but not enough to come out of my trance, for I did it again a hundred yards further on.

*

Jas, Frances and I were developing a talent for art. Connie also, but while I was being trained at school in the Ablett's System which confined us to drawing deck-chairs in every position with exact perspective, she was free and brilliant and expressionist. She and I spent days modelling in bas-relief in plasticene.

Phil had a passion for music. An upright piano was put into our mad drawing room which had also acquired some cheap modern armchairs and so had become senselessly ugly. There was a harmonium for him in the dining room and he practised every spare minute. I was learning the piano but never could play anything however hard I tried. But from now onwards till near middle age I had so much purely physical energy that I was driven to spend most of my time just getting rid of it. My outlets in Southport were the gymnasium, the hockey field and the swimming baths, the two latter providing me with a kind of bliss—even the hockey field! I suppose a yearling foal galloping about its meadow feels something of the same. The delights of the swimming bath are more understandable as they foreshadow the glories of the sea. I had picked up a slim little girl who was a Junior Diving Champion from Australia, whose arrow-like flights I tried to imitate with my much broader and heavier body and splash. I was never elegant but was ambitious enough to scorn the top diving platform and dive off the railing of the gallery. The bath had its poetry. The domed glass roof collected and re-echoed the screams of young voices in a sound that was the quintessence of excitement. As one entered the turnstile and started down the long salt-smelling corridor, the sound was heard rising in the distance like a choir of ecstatic angels. The smell of coconut matting soaked with brine was unique, and coming out at the end of the corridor one saw the shaken pale green water that was always trying to restore its broken surface. The shallow end was a thrashing mass of young bodies, but the deep end was less used and there was a pleasure in waiting for it to smooth out before one pierced it with a dive. If, as often happened, I was the last to leave the water toward closing time, I could watch the whole water of the bath slowly settle. The green tiles and white pointing of the bottom would reach toward a restored pattern, wildly feeling at first through jig-saw disturbance for their missing lines, quivering as these found their place, then showing a kind of placid breathing before absolute stillness held them. With what loving reluctance I left that immaculate calm!

In the summer we were back at Arnside, and there we swam daily in the river, but as the currents were so dangerous we were always accompanied by Mother sitting most anxiously in a boat with one of our boatmen friends holding the oars. Nurse waited on the shore with towels to wrap us up as we came out blue with cold. Jas used to swim far out on the deadly tide and just had to be trusted to live. Except for her troubled face Mother showed no sign of worry. It may have been her heroism, but she did not know the river as I did.

*

In the house at the top of Garrett's path owned by Mother's family were our cousins on her side. Their mother was so unlike ours that we never thought of them as sisters. It was impossible to imagine them in the same nursery. None of us took after Mother in any way. It is a wonder how she could have given birth to so many without passing on a trace of her blood. She was as much a stranger among us as she had been among Father's family. This feeling worked both ways. As we grew up she looked at us with disappointed rejection. The cousins on her side were even more alien to us. We were like black and red ants. Many of the Wood cousins were very odd but we accepted them all as our natural kin, loving many and laughing with tolerance at the freaks. Mother's many unmarried sisters were kind and good to us, but the relationship never took root. Mother was incomparably the best of them. She had a great and gentle dignity.

The cousins were inescapable holiday company. We had grown up practically without art or music but we were not Philistine by nature. The cousins were, though with one exception. They were large, fair and brawny. The three girls, older than any of us, were hideously prudish over bathing, hideously hearty in organising sports and picnics. In the evenings they had sing-songs when they sang the music hall hits of the moment of a vulgarity that shocked both my innocence and my ear. They were all rather condescending to our freakishness, to the way we dressed, to the way Mother let the household run itself. They endeavoured to 'help' us.

Fortunately there were too many of us to keep count of. I was off by myself in the woods most of the time, absorbing what has lasted me all my life. For a time we had Connie to stay with us. She and I lay together on the flowering turf or roamed at large. There was on the hill a grove of ancient yew trees well away from all paths. Here we took off our clothes and played Dryads for the pleasure of the breeze over our whole skin, and of watching the sun spots and leaf shadows playing over our smooth bodies. It was the most innocent thing imaginable and no Acteon burst in upon us and no shocked female reported us.

It was in this summer that a car entered the family circle. Till now none of our relations or friends had had one. My sister Mary, known to us as Grumps, startled us by becoming the first private owner. She bought a small car and somehow learned to drive. There were no schools nor driving tests. Probably this burst of enterprise was because horses gave her asthma. Early cars were open, and the hideous 'motoring cap', the least practical wear imaginable, was considered almost as essential as the steering wheel. Mary did not take any of us out with her. Mother used to say, 'Isn't Mary brave, alone with her car'. I used to enjoy the word 'with', as if the car were a personal enemy. I infinitely preferred a pony trap along narrow lanes between the blackberry hedges.

*

To counterbalance the joys of Arnside, holidays ended with visits to the dentist, always a place of torture in those days of crude instruments and no painkillers. As an example of the barbarities practised, Mary, whose front teeth projected slightly and rested on her lower lip (a frequent feature of Victorian faces and I imagine all Dickens' young ladies with it), instead of being fitted with a gold band to draw her teeth back, returned from the dentist with her front teeth sawn off halfway up and their still projecting thickness plated with gold. How she must have wept when she saw the ruin of her smile and remembered the agony she had endured! I think it was considered a blunder, for we changed our dentist. There were now two to choose from. Frances went to a handsome young man whom she found charming. He had protective ways, cradled her head and caressed her cheek, even perhaps kissed the pain better. (We always went alone.) I felt contempt for this kind of thing and preferred a grim disciplinarian called Mr Fitch. The very name suggests the action of that horrid little hooked tool. He was tall with enormous black eyes and an expression of icy bitterness. My eyes were enormous and black too, but they got no reaction from him. I was there to have my teeth seen to and inexorably that was going to be done. When after an eternity of pain the tears ran down my cheeks, he turned away for another implement saying contemptuously, 'What are you crying for?' At the end of the session by way of a come-back, I asked him if he could recognise his patients with their mouths shut? He passed over this impertinence, merely remarking that my teeth had a formation interesting to dentists and he would like a photograph of them. Released from the chair and the ordeal over, I returned home very cock-a-hoop and boasted to my mother that Mr Fitch wanted a photograph. She fell into a predictable panic and wanted immediately to push me into the arms of Frances's cuddler. To avoid this and keep my self-respect I had to explain he was interested in nothing but my teeth—didn't want the face they belonged to.

Frances, two years older than I, was given to kissing in corners and running away with girlish laughter. Connie had the same dentist as Frances and also a more amorous doctor, but her body was developing into a lure for men, a rounded sinuosity that Venus cannot have bettered. She took advances lightly and contemptuously, but without offence. I was still a young Touch-me-Not. Yet for Mother Frances could do nothing wrong. She was an ordinary sweet girl doing what real girls do, but with every year that I grew Mother watched me with growing concern. I was something she neither understood nor trusted.

3

When I was fifteen all the family were at boarding school except myself and Phil. He was wholly occupied by his music and even raised Mother's heart to the skies by playing the big chapel organ during the service. She longed for all the boys to become Wesleyan ministers, but to be an organist was new and welcome.

About this time, when I was much alone, my guardian's wife died, after barely three years of marriage. I could not bear the thought of his grief, and as his house was near my school I often looked in to see how he was, and found him quite desolate. He welcomed my young and unexpected sympathy and we became near to each other in a personal, not merely a family, relationship. I used to go to Chapel with him simply to be beside him so that he should not be alone in his pew. But the evening service breeds emotion as an overheated railway carriage breeds germs. We held each other's hands.

Ever since Father died, Mother could not bear to sleep alone. When we were all little we slept with her in rotation. There was a kind of promotion in sleeping in a big bed with French curtains and in a grownup's room. As the boys grew it had to be Frances or me. Now I was the only girl at home. It was no longer a ritual honour, 'Whose turn is it to sleep with Mother?' but had become a trap for scenes. To be held in someone's arms in bed for a scene is intolerable. Also Mother was neurotically nervous. Though all the house was locked, she still locked her bedroom door inside and had six-inch-long screws that fastened the sash windows, and a police whistle under her pillow. All for what? There was nothing to fear at all in those orderly days. I hated being locked and screwed in.

Mother had begun to brood about the White Slave Traffic and was sure Frances and I would be snatched. She warned me constantly till I was reduced to looking right and left if I even crossed our little street to the letter box, not, as moderns might think, for the traffic, but lest there should be—a nun! Nuns and parsons were the bogies in disguise, NEVER to be spoken to.

Mother had taken up 'rescue work' and was the only woman on the board of the workhouse, where her particular interests were the Children's Home and the young women who left their illegitimate babies there when they themselves came out. The Matron had been chosen by the all-male board and was a heartless painted Jezebel against whom Mother's black-clad quietness was powerless. I saw this creature once and was horrified that any children should be entrusted to her.

Mother took the emergent 'fallen' girls into her care. She even in reckless generosity took them into her house as servants hoping in that way to keep them straight. She had perhaps not thought that in the holidays this would involve her in a constant fear of her own sons, now nineteen and seventeen years old. She felt compelled to keep watch. There was a particularly sweet and attractive little thing polishing brass stair-rods throughout the house, who could not fail to smile at two handsome young men, who themselves might naturally think they were backing Mother up by behaving with kindness. But alas! Before long she told Frank she would rather see him dead than having anything to do with 'these girls'. This resulted of course in endless family mirth. The boys were outraged and all their jibes were directed at Mother, so tragically well meaning. Frances and I, not being under suspicion, had more sympathy with her and with the unfortunate girls. Frances in fact took on a protégée, a very lively red-haired girl of her own age who adored her, and who did afterwards 'go straight'. Mother explained to me the value she put on conventional behaviour. The strong must protect the weak. The strong must never do what for the weak would be dangerous. I rebelled entirely against this attitude. The term 'levelling down' had not yet come into use, but a socialism not in material things but in morals and behaviour I would not have. 'Nothing venture, nothing have' was more my ambition: flights, not canary cages. As time went on Mother's incomprehension of us increased; derision became our normal attitude in private, and in her presence silence, sometimes broken by an outburst of choking laughter. Jas was cruelly witty. Only Frances understood her, but she could never get on with the boys. For me on the contrary they had become the most important and loved persons in life, and I was now old enough to be received into their exclusive circle. Jas at Cambridge had become an aesthete, not yet a painter, and a great dandy. His good looks devastated any visiting girl. Frank was nervous and vulnerable but a very determined character. Phil was a charming mystery to whose mind the only clue was sudden engaging laughter.

Connie was still my special school companion (quite indifferent to the boys). She introduced me to *Tess of the D'Urbervilles* and *Jude the Obscure* which she loved for its pessimism but I hated. Both books were considered by our elders quite unfit to read. She was usually away in the holidays. After one such long absence, she confided to me that she was in love. The father of the family with whom she had been staying was, she told me with as much approval as any Georgette Heyer heroine, a notorious rake. He had made love to her, now sixteen, and without him she could not live. I listened with keen interest and sympathy as if to a novel, but was too young to guess that her love was a final and ferocious fact. I left her looking forward to their next meeting. I myself at last was sent to boarding school.

The school, Laleham, at which Mary and Frances had been

till now, was described to me by them as a kind of heaven from which I was excluded. There were many things from which I was excluded, such as visits to friends or relatives. When I asked why, my sisters replied, 'because you don't know how to behave'. As I didn't know how, I did not know what they meant, and still don't.

However, Laleham was now closed. Frances was to fill up two terms with me in a new school before going on to Paris to 'finish'. Such a liberal and worldly idea as Paris can never have arisen in Mother's head. It must have been suggested by the retiring Headmistress. No member of our family on either side had ever done such a thing, nor any Wesleyan of our acquaintance. In the meantime for Frances, to move to a new school at nearly eighteen was hard, especially as through ill health she had missed so much schooling and would be placed below her age, but it was not so desperately hard as it would be now. There were still no exams of any importance to our future life, but looking back I am surprised that Mother who loved Frances so particularly should not have guessed to what unhappiness she was sending her.

The school chosen for Frances and me was a small private one of sixty or so pupils run by a Quaker lady, therefore safe for our morals. It was in Sussex, where we might hope to correct our North Country accents.

We made the long train journey alone, crossing London, where I had never been before, in a growler, and then taking a stopping train, full of strange girls, to our destination. I was always a bad traveller and sat miserably beside an open window. The old trains had such luxuries as windows that could be let right down, out of sight inside the woodwork. There were notices saying IT IS DANGEROUS TO LEAN OUT OF THE WINDOW. One's head might be knocked off by a passing express. Nevertheless children always hung out as far as they could. The disadvantage was that we got covered with soot and the carriage seats all smelled strongly of it.

We arrived exhausted, and were relieved to find we were to

share a small bedroom and not be in a dormitory. This had been arranged because Frances, ever since her operation and burns, had terrible nightmares in which she screamed so that I could hardly bear it.

Next day we were shown round by a girl whose kindness was at first reassuring to the lost, but she turned out to be Marcia, that dreadful do-gooder in Ivy Compton-Burnett's *A House and its Head*. She was another Wesleyan and would therefore accompany us to the penance of the local Chapel on Sundays. The Chapel was like a small lecture room and the minister thought the sermon the most important part of the service, in which there was little to inspire devotions. His boring rigmaroles were always divided into five parts, firstly, secondly, thirdly, etc. with recapitulation, and were counted off before our eyes on his fingers, of which one was missing, so the Thirdly was always tapped on the remaining stump, waited for with revulsion.

The kindness shown by the do-gooding girl had been a surprise, but real life soon intruded. Among the elder girls there was one Dorothy, who by her snobbish style, ruled the school. I wonder how she came to be in a Quaker establishment. She was well dressed and groomed, with family bracelets and an exquisite wrist watch. She wore hand-made shoes on her elegant feet. She had a face that would command gallant attentions from members of the Hunt at a Meet, and an exaggerated accent of the kind we had been sent south to acquire. She was always surrounded by her satellites. On the first evening Frances and I, unselfconsciously dressed in home-made mistakes, sat in a corner of the classroom with our embroidery. Although totally unlike in character we were considered identical in appearance. Frances had a better complexion and blacker hair, and she had a smile whereas I only had a grin. We were of the same height and build and were instantly taken for twins. The dazzling group of senior girls led by Dorothy approached and sat round us. In my naiveté I mistook this for kindness and gladly answered all

Lucy, Frances, Frank, Mary, Phil and Jamie

Patty Ashton

the questions she asked, however impertinent. Many of my answers got an encore ('Say that again—so-and-so didn't hear') and were received with an alluring smile by Dorothy and nudges and giggles from the rest. Frances, older and wiser, remained mute. I was ebullient and feeling that I was being some sort of success. 'Where did you get your nice embroidered dress from? The embroidery on it is rather like what you are doing.' I answered all questions without embarrassment and my answers continued to lead to more. Finally the inquisitorial group broke into open mirth and began to repeat to each other my pronunciation of such words as ask, basket, path, bath, faster, etc. which had been carefully elicited by Dorothy. I now realise that a North Country accent had never been heard before by these Southerners (no broadcasting in those days) and was infinitely ridiculous. I found I rather gloried in it and was not at all put out. Later on we heard from our Chapel-going companion that Dorothy had given out that we were 'charity girls'. I now thought as little of Dorothy as she did of me, and was undisturbed. Consequently I was little ragged, but Frances became the butt of the crudest element in the school and was jeered at cruelly and lived in one long blush. We found ourselves much in the company of the other outstanding oddity who, like us, had no choice. She was the daughter of a diplomat in Constantinople, and gave the impression of being half Turkish; something of the harem hung about her, as if reared on Turkish Delight. She was tall, fat and stupid but utterly good natured. She had one brown eye and one blue, in a long melancholy oval face. She was mad with loneliness and received us with a surge of relief that was irresistible. She never learned to distinguish us one from the other. She liked to be stroked like a cat. Stroking was very fashionable that term, originating from the abominable Dorothy, whose satellites queued up for the privilege of stroking her arms and shoulders. When she left the school the practice vanished.

We were both homesick every minute of every day. When

Mother came to see us at half term it was for us rapture. She was as wildly loved that weekend as she ever could have hoped to be. After that we ticked off the days till we could go home, the cramp of the heart lessening day by day till floods of relief began to dizzy us.

At home again, the school uniform discarded, I rushed off to find Connie. She had written to me some time before to say that her mother had forbidden her to go to her cousin (whose father she loved) for the holidays, so I knew she would be at home. A shock awaited me. Her mother looking very strained let me in, saying only that Connie was in the drawing room. I wondered that she did not come to meet me, but went in. She lay inert on the chesterfield, looking into space. She neither smiled nor moved nor looked at me. She might have been in a coma except for the look of pain that stiffened her face. I tried to talk to her, but there was no response, I did not even know if she heard. I stayed about an hour looking with fright and incomprehension at this wreck of a friend. Her mother sat by her like her fate, helpless to do otherwise, frozen into patience. When I left she did not say, 'Come again'. She said nothing. It was obvious that this state of affairs was accepted as permanent as far as one could see. It made no difference to Connie if I was there or not. She wanted only one thing in the world and without it was as good as dead. I never went again, nor heard from Connie or her mother for many years, for they left Southport. I do not remember how we got in touch again, but at thirty Connie was still living with her mother 'so as not to grieve her'. She was beautiful, attractive and more remarkable than ever, but quite joyless. She told me how often she had tried to kill herself as if by convincing accident, but had always failed. When her mother died, Connie committed suicide by gas, not out of grief but because she could at last do so without causing grief. I have been ashamed all my life that when Connie was broken I found nothing to do for her.

*

Our guardian continued always to do every possible kindness. He now suggested that Frances and I should take it in turn to spend the weekend with him. He still had the two devoted servants trained by his late wife and the house was kept up in its previous style. It was a great change from ours, now so lapsed and as shoddy as Mother's indifference could make it. Her meals were meagre. I remember my shame when we had a friend of Patty Ashton's to dinner. The food set before her was yellow haddock stewed in milk in a brown pie dish, followed by another identical pie dish containing yellow-skinned baked custard. I remember too the boys' angry muttering when the midday meal was one small pot of potted meat for seven people with thin bread and butter, followed by milk pudding. Mother may have been hard up, but money was never mentioned in the family. At our guardian's every meal was a work of (Dutch) art, ample and perfect and served with the style it deserved, presented to us with reverent ritual by a silent waitress, herself an august figure. Probably these weekends gave us some idea that social manners existed. At home there was only Mother's severe simplicity to copy. When once she invited a lady of importance on some committee to dinner and finger bowls were actually put on the table, Phil, taking his place and reviewing the scene, said in his broadest Lancashire, 'What's them basins?' The meal was, not surprisingly, a calamity.

*

Though Mother had no friends of her own except the faithful Patty Ashton, she welcomed any of our cousins and they loved her for her gentleness. They all had more difficult parents to suffer from. For instance, when Aunt Emily reigned alone at Woodbank, Father's younger brother, Uncle Peter Fred, used to bring his family to Southport for Christmas. In him, all Father's dynamism had turned into passionate neurosis. His wife had been tall, elegant and very kind, but she died early and thereafter all his crankiness rioted unchecked. His family all spoke of him with frustration and despair. They were half a generation older than we were and Peter Fred was a blight on all their lives. One daughter had been turned out and cut off absolutely for becoming a Roman Catholic. The eldest daughter who kept house for him had become a physical wreck, but she had such an explosive fund of feeling that she never stopped talking and could not speak at less than the highest pressure. She thus made a perpetual joke of herself, but never resented laughter.

There were three sons: the eldest, Norris, was very tall (his implacable father hardly came up to his breast pocket) and as beautiful as his mother. He was a scholar and an aesthete with a passion for the military, which in those days was not at all incompatible. When he bent from his great height to offer a cheek to his young cousins, Frances and I agreed in this at least, that we received an overwhelming honour. He was the paragon of the family. Alas, in the First World War at Gallipoli those splendid legs were shot away, and he died with serene dignity in the presence of his brother Wilfred. In my early school days Wilfred was a young doctor. He was not good-looking but had great charm, especially with children. His yearly arrival was looked forward to with ever increasing interest as we grew older. The youngest son, about Jas's age, was a merry tragic-clown with a passion for music.

Aunt Emily, so much more regal and expansive than her sisters, gave a Christmas party yearly for the assembled Woods. There was no Christmas tree, nor Christmas presents other than a florin each, but things were done with a kind of ritual splendour. Although she lived alone in the big house, she somehow kept up a standard of food worthy of the previous generation. She gave us a splendid evening feast with all the family silver in evidence down the long table. Uncle Peter Fred, whatever his domestic faults, had warm formal manners in family gatherings, and he did not forget his nephews' and nieces' names.

After the feast we went into the library for prayers, taken by him. We sat round on Chippendale chairs whose red leather seats may have been original. They were so worn and crumbly that the colour came off on my party frock of white broderie anglaise. Unexpectedly perhaps, the reading of the Christmas passages of the New Testament was for me the greatest joy of the evening. Peter Fred had a thrilling personal voice and read superbly, looking down at the Scriptures through pince-nez set crookedly on his nose and his chin thrust out in affirmation. It might have been actually happening as he read. Every year it was exactly the same and always I trembled. Even today whenever I hear 'Now when Jesus was born in Bethlehem of Judea in the days of Herod the King' it is Peter Fred I hear, and am back in that gathering.

When the reading was over, we turned to kneel in front of our chairs, all except Mother and Aunt Emily who allowed themselves to bow their heads seated. I was unhappily aware that I presented, if only to heaven, a bottom dyed rosy-pink. Peter Fred had also his own fascinating style of prayer compounded of the Authorised Version and his own imagination. Who but he would have thought of voicing, 'May thy church prosper O Lord, and *do exploits*'?* In what other context do these words occur? They have come down the years with me, and now when I come in exhausted after too much digging in the garden I think contentedly, 'I have *done exploits*'.

On a much later occasion, as Wilfred and I knelt at adjacent chairs, we were publicly prayed for with ominous foreboding, ending 'Let them not lean unto their own understandings'. The shudder of Wilfred's knees on the floor boards was relayed to mine and bound us together.

Our other cousins were the Boston family, where as a small child I went to my first party and met my future husband. They had a very big house at the far end of the town so that we only began to see them regularly when we were old enough to walk there on our own. The father had five children

* Later traced to Daniel XI, 28-32.

(69)

by his first wife, and after her death he married our cousin (on the Wood side) and had seven more. It was again an Ivy Compton-Burnett household (with what fiendish accuracy she describes the family life of her youth!), with the tensions between the two families and all the hierarchies of age groups, ending upstairs where the two youngest were segregated until in their teens because their mother could not endure an empty nursery. It was a hotbed of aggravation and unbridled laughter, mostly directed at the parents. The father emerging from his study, or at the head of the table, sang out his musings, moralistic or apprehensive, with a burst of false amusement at the end. He had a trick of puffing out and deflating his cheeks after speaking as if simultaneously to apologise for what he was saying and to approve of himself. I do not see fathers doing this now. They have all been put in their place by their children, but it was a period trick. It would be impossible to read aloud the sayings of the father in Ivy Compton-Burnett's *Men and Wives* without this deprecating self-puff. There was nothing so silly this cousin would not say it, and his outbursts were the joy of his family. Perhaps less the joy of his second wife. She was a very odd character. She was stout, but her very handsome features had never thickened, they were as finely cut as if sculpted in wood, and as immobile. However in this set face her great eyes blazed. She took no part in anything and seldom spoke except perhaps a short burst of irritation that nobody took any notice of. She had no influence on what went on except to oppose change. It was an inertia that went far beyond indolence. She wore the same clothes for every occasion as long as I knew her and the same comfortable old shoes. She had strong prejudices and kept to all the rules of normal good manners—where at a Christmas party of thirty everyone should sit, which uncle should be asked to say Grace, which to carve etc.—and though sympathetic was terrified of showing it; her thoughts never surfaced. I now think that perhaps she was entirely made up of passions, imaginations and fears so contradictory that all movement was cancelled. At any rate she produced a vital and handsome family far more intelligent than their father. When the latter was more than usually outrageous she reddened and tore at the neck of her blouse. There was a family legend that whenever a child was being born to him, he paced the house in a frenzy lamenting, 'Never again! Never again!' But promptly a year later there was another, and the remorseful vow was repeated. He had a lugubriously tolerant sex mania and seemed to expect incestuous goings on. When Hide and Seek was being innocently played he patrolled the bedrooms intoning, 'Beds again. Beds again.' And if he had a bad day at the office, he would look down the long tea table stretched before him, lined with young expectant faces, and prophesy that he would live to see his daughters on the streets. In such a house one could count on tumult and humour all the time.

I do not know how this big handsome house was kept going. Most likely it was all done by their old family nurse (who also brought me into the world). She was a tiny withered person of iron will and much tolerance. At the age of eighty she still worked there, assisted by a dear old butler of the same age, who carried in trays of thirty plates above doddering legs. The nurse, among her other uses, in term time slept on eight mattresses to keep them 'aired' under her old bones, a typical idea in a house not run by reason.

The children of the first family were unlike their gypsyish siblings. Three girls came first. The eldest was perhaps six when her mother died, and I suppose much can be implanted in a child by that age. Otherwise they were all brought up in the same household as the second family. Nevertheless they achieved as it were out of themselves, a grace, a culture, and a dignity all their own. They were Tennysonian. I loved them all dearly, as did all the second family. They were wholly good in the biggest sense and with it had both humour and charm. I have met only two others I could put beside them. Their kind does not happen in the modern climate. Harold whom I was later to marry was the youngest. His mother had died at his birth, for which reason his father disliked him and always treated him unfairly. He resembled his sisters physically, but he had a daemon of his own among the excellences.

*

The next term Dorothy and her cronies had left, as also our *faute-de-mieux* harem cat. There was room to expand. More important to me than all the drawbacks of school was that I was at last in contact with the real sea (heard all night in the bedroom), that savagely demolished the groins built in close rows down the pebble beach. The infinitely varied clamour of inrush and ebb is to me the most comforting sound one can hear. A trout stream has more grace notes but it lacks the fugal strength of the sea. Inland were the smooth downs where in summer the chalk showing through the grass gave the earth a luminosity which on a blue day made it akin to the sky. Sea and downs were the great and real benefit of the school to me. It had no other, but these were inestimable. As our education was paid for out of the money we each should inherit at twenty-one, no extras were denied us. We rode over those uniquely beautiful downs, still unspoilt with their ancient dew ponds and tracks bordered with gorse. There was nothing military about the riding lessons. The old man who escorted us had outlived any keenness he ever had. We could on a fine day dismount and tether the horses while we stretched and lazed at ease in a place of equal secrecy and vista, and imagined what we would. There was an old race course where the overworked horses could gallop flat out if they had it in them. I had big bones and puppy-fat, so I was always given a strong roan, good to ride. We all of course rode side-saddle, but no style was expected of us. Long streaming hair added to the pleasure of a gallop, echoing the horse's mane and tail. It had of course to be plaited and tied up again before the decorous trot back through the town. The old man willingly helped. Then there was sea bathing. Over the steeply shelving beach big waves sidled along the groins and in retreating dragged shoals of pebbles across our shins. Trained as I was in the strong currents of a tidal wave, I was happy and reckless in this cleaner and more exhilarating rough and tumble. When in singing class we had Kipling's 'Sussex by the Sea', I was wholly at one with him.

Sometimes on fine Sundays the school was allowed to take the long walk across Hindhead to the little church at Alfriston. Chapel girls were allowed to pocket their presumed prejudices and join in with the others. Alfriston was then a tiny mediaeval village with one half-timbered inn and the old church. I do not remember its architecture, but under the central tower the bellringers pulled and swung in full view of the congregation, a splendid start to what to me was an eye opener. It was my first experience of an ordered ritual, no impertinently familiar, sentimental impromptu prayers, but all in majestic English. The psalms were exactly what one would wish to sing, the General Confession what one needed to say, the Litany not a word too long for me. Why must they now alter that masterpiece and make it 'everyday' and for 'the common man' when to a young person used to current commonplace and coming across this for the first time it seemed overwhelmingly beautiful? I nursed it in my heart.

*

At school on Sunday evenings the Headmistress took a kind of abridged Evensong. This took place in the dining room with the tables pushed to one side and the chairs in rows. The dining room was bare and bleak, its only decoration two very small prints of Burne-Jones' 'King Cophetua and the Beggar Maid', and Turner's 'Fighting Temeraire' *in sepia*! (If any art was taught in this school I have no recollection of it. My only educator was Jas.) Nevertheless, perhaps because we had all spent the afternoon writing home, Sunday evening managed to have that creepy, soapy, Now-the-day-is-ended feeling inescapable from all 'observed' Protestant Sundays. We sang the fixed psalms and also the psalms for the day in

(73)

full. We also said the Creed. It so happened that one evening a girl whose conscience had perhaps been troubling her, or perhaps she had just decided where in the dining room the East lay, turned and bowed during the Creed to the surprise of the school. The following Sunday before the service the Quaker Headmistress announced in a grimly disapproving voice that the worship of the heart was quite sufficient and she must ask her pupils not to indulge in unnecessary gestures and automatic practices. Nevertheless, in the Creed, the same girl repeated her bow and the girl beside her half did so. In three weeks the whole school was turning and bowing, including myself. I heartily approved, quite apart from having been bred to be a martyr (though on the other side). Surprisingly there was no reaction from the Headmistress. She accepted defeat.

It is just possible she consulted the head girl, whom I will attempt to describe.

The leader of the school was now Eileen. She was tall and graceful with light blue eyes and a high brow topped with baby curls. She was potentially intellectual had there been any scope for it. She carried herself superbly and unselfconsciously. There was nothing dominating about her face. Her chin retreated just far enough to allow her pretty teeth to rest lightly on her lower lip in that smile that the dentist had so cruelly sawn off poor Mary. Her manner was entirely playful, her snubs final. She was intriguing, very secret, very selfish and utterly charming—a Millamant. I, her junior, admired from afar, astonished by so much presence and *savoir faire*. Eileen could do what she liked with the Headmistress. An approving school watched her at it. The Head was bewitched but did not see it. She proudly doted on Eileen. Whenever in my long life I have heard or read of an intriguing Court lady or irresistible enchantress I see Eileen as the only imaginable incarnation. Although so popular, Eileen had only one friend, the next most attractive girl in the school, much younger than herself and of the opposite type, a sort of elfin gypsy, very magnetic, with the delicate limbs and huge black eyes of a gazelle. Though in a different dormitory she was often in Eileen's bed against the most stringent rule. Every girl knew, nobody censured. These two were of a quality to do what they chose. For my part, I thought nothing of it, I had never heard of lesbianism. I knew beds as the best place for friendship and confidences, and perhaps the younger one was homesick. Perhaps they were old family friends. Was Eileen good or was she wicked? She could have been either, or both, which is much more frequent. She was then eighteen, and I have never seen or heard of her since. I here acknowledge her.

Many years later I met her gazelle again. She was dance hostess with a travelling jazz band and was as sad as an old shoe.

*

Frances was soon removed from what must have been for her a place of torture. She went to Paris from where she wrote me rapturous letters. I now slept in a dormitory with eight beds. We had curtained cubicles and were not supposed to enter each other's. Under each bed was a shallow enamel bath. It was the rule that we must pour cold water over ourselves every morning. There was a fat lazy girl who never combed her hair though it was very fine and long. Some instinct for bullying persuaded me I ought to keep up the standards, so every morning I poured water over her shrinking baby-soft flesh, cheered on by all the others, and I set about her hair that looked as if mice were nesting in it. Before it was sleek half of it was out. After that it was less trouble. I do not think she bore me any illwill. Probably at home it had always been done by a firm Nanny.

I was going up in the school, soon to be captain of games and head girl in place of Eileen. I enjoyed all to myself a sixth form. The Headmistress had yielded to the ambition of sending a pupil to the university. It was still an ultra-modern idea. When my brother Jas, himself a convention breaker at

Cambridge, heard of it he was appalled. 'It must be Oxford. I couldn't live down a sister at *Girton*.' I had no ambition. Formerly they had tried to make me a missionary, now it was to be a 'blue-stocking'. However, I did not mind the idea of Oxford. I liked Latin and loved Greek. The mistress who had this unexpected job given her was not, I think, quite up to it, but there were only the two of us and we sat in the sun and read the *Odyssey*.

The Head, perhaps intoxicated by the grandeur of being able to say on the prospectus 'Pupils prepared for the universities', also introduced a Master to give history lectures. The school was assembled and crowded into the large classroom. When we were all seated and expectant, in strode a young man in cap and gown. I suppose he might have been twenty-one, but to us he was adult, a large MAN, brawny and not bad-looking. Confronted with sixty pairs of unwavering female eyes he soon broke into a sweat and his hands shook. Throughout his lecture, on the English Constitution, delivered with eyes desperately unfocused on the middle distance, he continually mopped the large drops of sweat running down his brow. At the end—or perhaps before he got to it—he turned and stumbled out, only not running, all dignity lost. As he left the room a roar of chatter broke out which he must have heard as he fled. Once was enough for him.

There was also a young woman new on the staff. (There were seven resident teachers in all.) She was very plain and therefore extra vulnerable, and pathologically shy. She taught the juniors, not me. Her class was always in an uproar, their object being to make her weep, in which with horrid ingenuity and co-operation they succeeded. This is the only time in my life when I have seen mass female cruelty in action. They looked forward to it. Wretched young woman, like the hen all the others peck and the cock never notices!

I was a poor successor to Eileen. I was too fat for beauty, too ill-dressed and too uppish. I had a quick eye for home-sickness and with the young and the lost I had a loving relationship, but I was never popular either with the girls or the staff. I asked a mistress whom I met after I had left school, why the staff from top to bottom had such a down on me? She said, 'Because you always looked so defiant. It was very annoying to us.'

Many people complain now of the hostility of teenagers, but I had no consciousness of any such feeling, only of the need to protect something not yet clear to me. Perhaps there was a natural arrogance, but of that I am not able to judge. I suppose arrogance is always unconscious. In my last term I made a few friends. Probably the head girl, even if she has no special charisma, always has a few adherents.

The entrance examination for Somerville took me to Oxford for the first time. Of course I was bewitched. The only towns I had been in up to now were Southport and Bootle! The entrance paper appalled me when I read it through. It was at once clear that I had received no education. There seemed to be nothing I had ever heard mentioned, let alone knew anything about. The only question I now remember was, 'What was Shakespeare's idea of Woman?' which struck me as so silly that I said so, and wrote quite a lot with vigour. I wrote some rubbish on other questions since one had to cover a few sheets. Normally I had enjoyed exams. I liked the quietness and tension, the extreme orderliness and the piles of new inviting paper. It was like a good parlour game and often I have minded the results of these more. I was not much troubled in this case. I had no personal feeling involved. I was only obliging other people. However, in those days there was no competition and greatly to my surprise I was accepted.

4

There was a year to wait before I could go to Somerville, during which time I was to go to Paris. It was in the summer holidays after leaving school that my gentle and nervous mother became Public Enemy No. 1. Every summer now she rented an empty school house at Arnside where there was room for any school friends or cousins. Nurse was now acting as housekeeper and fed us abundantly. She took on all the work, which must have been heavy. Mother never suggested we should do anything to help. It was never thought of. Mother was only interested in the morals of the serving class, not their comfort. In the Aunts' house nearby were all the cousins on Mother's side.

Wilfred Wood usually stayed with us at Arnside. He had in previous summers taught us young rabbits to play tennis—a great test of good nature. He took us all for long moonlight walks through the woods and chilled our blood with stories of were-wolves. When he was with us the conversation at meals was lively and preposterous for he had a bubbly sense of humour and mimicry. Patty Ashton's slender pink hand was folded over her nose to contain her shaken giggles. All the girls, in both families Wood and Boston, loved him and almost any of them would have married him, but it took him nearly twenty years to decide. Perhaps at this time Frances and I were in the lead. Frances was rather delicate which gave me a further advantage. Wilfred liked twenty-mile walks over the fells which the boys seemed not to want; that left me as a possible companion. Before he came I had been in the habit of climbing out of my bedroom window in the early dawn to go for long rambles by myself, coming back at breakfast time before anyone noticed.

Wilfred and I spent long days together walking over the map. One does not talk much while climbing uphill, and going down it is the sheer exhilaration and the new view that takes one's attention. The day's exertions were on the whole silent, friendly and detached. One hot day, resting on the turf of a high point, overlooking Windermere, Wilfred lay with his head heavy on my lap. I took this as a great honour, accepted in silence and surprise; but once home again I succumbed to the desire to confide my pleasure. I chose Mary whose grumpy reserve seemed safe, to whom I said, 'Wilfred lay with his head on my lap. I think he must like me.'

It would be difficult to imagine a more innocent confidence, but Mary hurried to Mother with dire warnings. Could it have been jealousy? She was so disastrously plain it never occurred to me she might have romantic feelings.

The next day Wilfred told me with embarrassment that Mother had asked him not to take me for walks again. This was monstrous and wounding. Wilfred was the safest company imaginable and the understanding between us was perfect. I blazed, speechless in fury. Why had Mother spoken to him behind my back and not to me? What reason had she for such stupid, unfair interference?

Worse was to come. It had for a long period of hot weather become a family habit to sleep out of doors, all of us, girls and boys, in serried ranks on the small back lawn, each of us on our ground sheet with what bedding we chose to take. The garden was closely surrounded by oak trees and hazel, leaving above our heads a circle of sky of that wonderful blue which cannot properly be called dark because it is star-lit all through to as far away as one can imagine, luminous and illimitable, across whose face shooting stars flew in curves. Or was it we on the earth who sped? My pallet was next to Wilfred's and on his other side the eldest of the Boston girls, now perhaps thirty, and a special friend of mine. Before settling to sleep, Wilfred was pointing out to me the stars overhead. He knew them all, and I till then had hardly known they had names, except the Pole Star; they were just 'The infinite shining heavens'. It was thrilling to know that every one of that receding hugeness was named. While my lesson was continued in whispers so as not to disturb the dormitory, poor Mother was peering through her bedroom window seeing evil where none was, even disturbing Patty Ashton, who never thought any evil, to come and see for herself.

In the morning stern words were said. I was told I must never put myself next to Wilfred again. I must sleep as far away as the garden allowed, or stay indoors. Disgust and contempt were my reactions. Did innocence not exist for her? My rejection of the insult was violent enough to set me on a course of outrageous and defiant unconventionality whenever opportunity offered. I have no doubt I left her with a real teenage flounce, and sought the company of my brothers, with whom I shared a world of candour, trust and decency. We had no fears for each other's behaviour.

Rain prevented me from having a chance to flout the embargo and Wilfred's holiday came to an end.

*

Mother must have retained from her early married days an unconscious hostility to and suspicion of the Woods as a race alien to her. At Arnside now her sister and family were in the other house a few hundred yards away. She preferred her walks with Patty Ashton and Frances. She can have had no special affection for this sister. A short cut to the river was down through the cousins' garden. I undressed there for bathing and raced down the zig-zag woodland path in my 'bathing dress' which was very decent, an all-over garment and even skirted. Bikinis were two world wars away. Our girl cousins in this athletic family were square, muscular and manly, but they went down to the river wrapped in long cloaks of towelling which they dropped only at the water's edge and instantly immersed themselves up to the neck however shallow the water. They were grievously shocked by my up-standing immodesty. They did not stand on the bows of a boat to dive, even less could they have considered the undignified climb up into the boat with its moment of bottom upwards. They tried to teach me decency, something Mother had never thought of till she found her little ones grown into dangerously sexed creatures. When these rather horrific female cousins had staying with them a baby girl one year old and were giving her a bath, a brother coming into the room was driven out with screams and would have been beaten had he persisted. Such dirty modesty is perhaps the result of experience.

Jas liked, admired and laughed at the father of this house for his rolling self-confidence and gusto. He had the twinkling little eyes of a porker. They now took notice of me. After a few displeasing signals of his intentions, he one day caught me on the landing and carried me fighting like a bull-calf into a bedroom where he flung me on to the bed and his twenty stone on top of me. From this extremity I was rescued by one of his sons calling his father to order. The old man was not put out of countenance. 'Ah well. All right, my boy.' Neither man seemed to think it out of the ordinary.

A few days later when Mother wished to send me with a message to her sister, I refused to go, saying Uncle was too dangerous. He wouldn't let me alone.

'Nonsense, you silly child,' she replied. 'It's only Uncle's way.'

This was her side of the family and therefore perfectly conformable. But she was right—it was Uncle's way, and there was to be no help from her.

*

That autumn I went to Paris. I did not find it the paradise described by Frances, but she had made a great friend there whom she brought home, an exquisitely dressed girl with a dramatically sensuous face, suitable I thought for a Borgia.

Her skin was as white as a camellia and her full curved lips rose red. She had a fascinating stammer and a snobbish background. It was probably our long deprivation of anything but dressmaker-made black that made Frances and me fall so deeply for sophisticated style. This girl was an exotic flower in our sterile soil at home. While Frances and I admired her strange beauty, she fell for Jas like Salome for John the Baptist, and failing him for Phil. Jas's taste was for simple uneducated beauties. He and Phil fled from her. Not surprisingly, she also had parent trouble.

I was less lucky in Paris. The other girls were amiable enough but not noticeable. There were two wealthy Canadians interested only in the shops, a plump little suburban puss and a lean pallid Anglo-Indian. The others, if any, have faded right out. Mademoiselle, who took us in for a living, was small and sour, porridge-skinned with blackcurrants for eyes. Her pension was in Neuilly near the Porte Maillot, where horse-drawn carriages waited instead of taxis. Imagine Paris without a taxi! In the morning piping shepherd boys came up the avenue with their goats, but in the night there were noisy sewage pumps, for these handsome houses had no proper main drainage. A stinking shaft ran down the centre of the house, with a closet and seat on each floor, without a flush.

We had halfhearted French lessons in the morning, obligatory but un-considered, and every afternoon Mademoiselle did her duty by taking blank English misses round the museums and monuments. I was breathless with excitement in the Louvre, but no guidance or information was offered. Paris made its mark on us according to what each one was prepared to see. Sometimes instead of Mademoiselle, we were chaperoned by a wan young widow drooping under the weight of her voluminous black crêpe. Her spiritless misery failed to rouse any response but impatience. I wonder now if perhaps it was that cold biting Hell that I have known since. At the time I judged it a weak misery, a feeble despair. She never spoke, but merely followed along with us. Mademoiselle, on the other hand, though without taste or intelligence, was not weak. She and I had disliked each other at first sight and it grew to detestation. Had my mother written to her about me, or was there something about me that enraged? True, I was nakedly naive, had no demureness, and no boundaries; but I also knew no evil unless pride in one's personal honour is evil. One day I had bent to stroke a friendly dog in the park, and had exchanged a word with its owner, a little man rather like it. Mademoiselle was scandalised. Thereafter whenever we walked, as we left the garden she gripped me by the wrist, holding me in leash as if to announce to all the men we passed that I would be after them if she let go. The humiliation was an intolerable wrong. Between us down our arms riveted at the wrist ran in both directions currents of hatred. We could have murdered each other like rats.

My letters home were full of complaints that no one was teaching me either French literature or French history, except at lower school level; but in spite of the fact that neither Mademoiselle nor the other girls thought these subjects any reason for a stay in Paris, I managed to get a fairly good grasp of the language. Even Paris did not teach me to dress.

*

In the Christmas holidays I was glad to be back again with my brothers, though Jas's affection took the form of cruel criticism, doubtless well deserved. His name for me was Bouncing Lulu. I thought the three of them the beauties and wonders of the world, though their manners especially to Mother shocked me. Jas was always derisive, but openly, which allowed her to feel it was backed by affection. His pet name for her was 'Mrs Foul'. It shocked Frank profoundly, but not me, because there was a sort of tenderness in his tone. The boys would have nothing to do with Frances. They said she was Mother's spy. I couldn't see it. There was nothing to spy on.

The boys were indeed very good-looking, and as most girls at eighteen have at least a brief blossoming into beauty, and as there was a strong family likeness especially between me and Jas, it is probable that I had my share of good looks. Phil was fair with light green eyes. He was more lightly built and his features were more incisive. He was still so silent that we knew no more of him than what we could see. He resembled a Byronic great great grandfather of whom we had an admired engraving.

As Frances and I were now physically grown up, we were allowed to share the bathroom with Mother. We learned with surprise that she had a beautiful body. She was taller than we were. Her skin was smooth and honey-coloured like the inside of a ripe melon. She had small breasts and long simple lines with never a crease. Who could have believed that under such graceless, ugly clothes there was such a delicate creature? It was a shock, and my affection for her instantly increased.

I spent the weekends with my guardian whose stable adult company and formal but warm manners were always a pleasure. Everything about him—his chapel-going, his relation with his mother, his county cricket, his deer-stalking, his salmon-fishing, his business (of which I never heard a word uttered, but it was wool) or his house—was controlled with easy precision. Nothing was out of order and his temper was perfectly equable. It was all superb. I loved the rich tobacco smell of the house, the quietness, the discreet gong. I loved the details of the furnishing, such as his great wardrobe in three divisions with shelves that slid out like drawers, with brass rails for rows of boots and shoes all with trees in them. It was as polished and ordered inside as it was out. My brothers' clothes were hung over chairs. There was no provision for a man in my mother's house, no trace left of Father's presence.

I liked the bathroom with its shining metal paraphernalia and its wealth of clean matching towels, its enormous perfect sponge. I enjoyed seeing him come out of it in the morning in his bathrobe with his hair wet and rubbed up on end, looking so lean and fit. I was getting very free in this house so different from our own. I'd never had a good morning kiss from a sort of Hector in a bathrobe before. I'm sure I gave every sign of a girl happy and at ease and without reserve. The inevitable happened. One evening his goodnight kiss was trembling and tender and my thoughtlessness collapsed into fright. What had I done? I was up against every woman's unsolvable dilemma, how to rebuff a man she dearly loves, how least to wound him. The very thought makes one tenderer and that again makes it harder.

Forgetting in my trouble all Mother's previous incomprehensions I told her what had happened, hoping for advice, not realising the inexorable cruelty of the situation. She said nothing, was neither sympathetic nor helpful, but a few days later she said she had told my guardian he was not to have me to stay alone again. I was getting too old and must have a chaperone. This again behind my back. It seemed an unexampled treachery after a confidence. She should of course have told me, but I see now that she relieved me of much embarrassment, and that he, being old-fashioned, would have thought it right and maidenly that I should talk to my mother. At the time I was as angry as wretched. I imagined he would think I had *complained*, a thought so unbearable that I could not again meet his eyes. I longed to rush to him and say, 'Anything whatever you could ever do is forgiven you in advance.' But he hadn't done anything. I was the silly fool. But I had no opportunity, and in fact seldom saw him alone afterwards, though years and years later we wrote to each other in terms as loving as before.

*

When I returned to Paris, this time it was with Jas. We went to a retired school teacher and his wife who took in young lodgers. It must have been one of my mother's ill-judged arrangements, for Jas of course if in Paris should have been at an art school. He and I shared a large private sitting room, but he got angry if any object of mine, such as my sewing, was visible in it. He couldn't live with other people's things. There were two other young men in the house who took lessons in French with Jas. The bad-tempered and ill-mannered teacher showed the greatest contempt for his pupils, as if they were the small boys he had formerly taught, but stupider, being English. It was a puzzle to me then and still is, how Jas came to be there and to put up with the insults. I on the other hand was perfectly free and could jaunt about as I wished, learning and loving the streets of Paris, though, except for museums and churches, what lay behind the façades was unknown. We never went to theatres or the opera, or restaurants or concerts, only to organ recitals at St Eustache or St Sulpice. One would think that a term in Paris with a brother such as Jas, then twenty-two, would be the most vivid and exciting period of my life. In fact it was constricted and quite unmemorable. I lived as young girls live from whom nothing is expected, aimlessly enjoying every minute of just being alive. Of the two other young lodgers, one was my age, very shy but agreeable company to share my long rambles. On cold, dark evenings we bought chestnuts roasted on braziers in the streets. The other was a gentle-manly half-wit who was Jas's chosen company. When I asked what he saw in him, he replied, 'He's like a China tea-pot that's perfect only that it doesn't pour'. The wife of our irritable host was good to me, even motherly in the accepting way my mother was not. We knew nobody outside the pension, no French friends ever dropped in on our hosts, no other French house was open to us. I had dropped overboard any ideas about education, was not conscious of missing anything. I ran round like a dog let off the leash. Nobody bothered me, nobody noticed me. Paris seemed without danger, just a lovely place to be in.

*

After this improbable interval I returned home and staved there for another half year, leaving Jas in Paris where he had found for himself a studio to study in, I think with Braque-mont, but can no longer be sure.

While I was at home, Harold began to visit us more often. He told me afterwards that Frances was the original attraction, but we took a cousinly interest in each other. Circumstances put him in our way. His father still resented him because of his mother having died at his birth. However large the second family grew year by year, revenge still had to be taken on the motherless boy, and it showed. He was cared for as an infant by a spinster aunt, more sentimental and possessive than a mother and irritatingly pathetic because she had not that elemental relationship. All her life Harold took it out of her for wanting to be loved as if she were his mother. At two years old he had a stepmother, who accepted him with kindness but immediately began to produce children like blowing bubbles. His father took him away from school at sixteen and put him in the family tannery as an ordinary workman to learn from the bottom. This was not thought necessary for any of the later sons who all went to the university. Tanneries have an indescribable stink which permeates everything and the hauling of hides out of the pits dyes the hands a permanent mustard tan. It was as this kind of young labourer that Harold visited us at the weekends, stinking and unglamorous, but he took it all with high spirits and no rancour. He was at this time in my story very immature, but his later characteristics showed. He was a little above average height but looked taller because of a small well-poised head of delicate bone structure. His hair was the colour of golden bread crust, silky and straight, his hazel eyes wide set and of a hawk-like alertness. His smile could be wicked or very sweet or both at once. He had a fiery, mobile and super-sensitive face. All his movements were highly personal, a curious mixture of secretiveness and eccentricity. To give an example of secrecy in movement, later on when I often waited for him in some hotel, I would watch the stream of men who pushed one after the other through the circular

(87)

swing door, never taking my eyes off it in the anticipation of seeing the loved head. Yet I never did see him enter; suddenly he would be beside me. Though so individual he had the faculty of disappearing in even a small crowd. With an ordinary education he could have been a literary eccentric. He loved language and wrote the liveliest letters. But having had so little schooling, his originality was channeled into a savage sense of humour. So ill-treated a young man was naturally received with warmth.

About this time the phonograph found its way into the world. Harold and I shared Schubert's Unfinished Symphony, wheezed and scratched out on the primitive machine. I was deeply moved, but Harold only said it was enough to make a dog flute.

*

I was in trouble again at home. The time had come for me to be formally received into the Wesleyan community. To Mother's horror, I refused. The last nail had been put in the Chapel coffin for me by a friend of Mary's at a prayer meeting. There is always at such functions a horrid silence at first when one begins to wonder what will happen if nobody prays at all. The embarrassment was courageously broken by the young lady saying in a prissy voice, 'Lord, make us winsome for good'.

I don't know how the rest of the family got over this stile. Perhaps they all went through it automatically at their respective Wesleyan boarding schools, with the whole of their class. I was subjected to all possible pressures. Mother's grief was unremitting. In bed at night she clasped me in her arms and wept, 'How can I meet your father on the other side when he asks me "What of the children?" How can I say to him "They are all safe except your darling, your little pigeon. She is lost"? ' I endured it with misery and revulsion. Who dared say I was lost? It was of course sad that she was tormenting herself, but it was idiotic. I was sent to regular private sessions with the minister. He used Mother's sorrow as his main argument, but also reasoned, coaxed and threatened. To his credit he did not try loving charm. Throughout my youth, as I was always interested in religion, I suffered from parsonical squeezing of knees and waist. Nonconformist Anglican and Catholic all astounded me by this approach. The last was a priest officiating in a French hospital in the war. I had asked him to explain the mass to me. He got out all the holy vessels, and with the chalice on his knee, for which I, an outsider, felt great reverence, he got down to cuddling.

Now at home I would not be moved. Yet as I stepped out of the fold into the unknown I repeated privately to myself, 'He shall keep my soul until that day'. I knew I was in search, not in denial. The abandonment of one's father's faith is a deep fear and sorrow and I felt an outsider.

5

The First World War broke upon us when we were all at Arnside. Jas, who had moved from Paris to Munich, had to return. Frank was a medical student at Cambridge, Phil had just left school. Harold was with us this year. He had become my natural companion. Cars were now in. They were the new thing to have. All the boys except Jas, who in all his life never learned to drive, had motor bikes which competed with the opening war in the excitement and stir. Mother took the war gallantly. She was buoyed with uncritical patriotism, swallowed all propaganda—as did I—and was prepared for the brave death of her sons. Otherwise her daughters might be raped. Her sister, with one son more to lose, was what Georgette Heyer would call a watering pot. The tears ran down her face all day and every day. Village patriotism decided that the wooden viaduct must be guarded day and night. From what? Bombers were in their infancy, not yet heard of, and parachutists not invented. The weeping mother saw her youngest set off to spend a night on the viaduct (unarmed) as if she would never see him again. There was no wireless, we only had the daily paper. All enlistment was voluntary, but good mothers did not doubt their sons would go. In our house there were no tears, but considerable tension and the inclination to roar about on motor bikes for tomorrow we die. Frank, Harold, Phil and I made long excursions up and down the Kirkstone pass or anywhere that offered engine tests rather than ease. I travelled in Frank's rickety sidecar, which meant my getting out to run up the hills after him as the engine would not take the weight up a gradient, or sometimes on the carrier of Harold's bike, which afterwards became my normal transport. Later still he gave me a superseded two stroke model and I buzzed around by myself, an incompetent and unthinking menace.

After a fortnight of merrily postponing the war, Harold announced that he was going to join up instead of going back to the tannery. His family were in Wales, where he would go to say goodbye to them. Frank and I decided to go with him. Mother strongly objected. It was too far, we might not get there in a day. We might break down on the way. Where in that case would we sleep? Thoughtlessly I replied, 'Anywhere. On the beach if it isn't raining. One can sleep anywhere.'

'*On the beach*? Oh no, no. What if you were seen?'

'Well, what if?'

There was a paralysed silence, then she went on—'There is something—I often wonder whether it wouldn't be better to tell you, but I don't know what is best to do. Something very dreadful once happened in the family. Something—I can't tell you. I am afraid it might make you worse.'

Worse than what, I thought. What am I supposed to have done? I guessed she must be referring to that Auntie Bertie of whom there was never any mention, nor photograph, who apparently never lived and never died, but who was the only one who had been kind to Mother. It would of course be the most generous one who went wrong.

Wringing her hands, which she often really did, Mother rushed from the room. She had of course gone to seek out Harold. He came to me looking dumbfounded. She had made him promise not to let me go with him 'because, she said, you can't be trusted'. Oho, I thought, I can't, can't I? To him I said he couldn't promise for me behind my back and I was coming with him in Frank's sidecar. So off we all went. The white dust off the unsurfaced roads was so smothering that my eyes were red and watering for days afterwards, but we arrived safely with the Boston family. Harold left the next day, seen off on the road by his eldest step-brother and myself. We watched him on his motor bike diminish in size and sound along the coast road. I shed no tears, but his brother did, turning to me confidingly with blurred eyes. I was grateful to him for weeping in my stead. I didn't go back with Frank to Arnside but stayed with my cousins.

*

That autumn I went up to Somerville, having got myself for once almost well dressed as I can see from photos, but my evening clothes were wild. My ideas were all à la Scheherazade. I bought luscious silks and chiffons and had them made up to my own design or made them myself. I remember them well but can't imagine what I looked like in them. Mother must have been startled by the unlikely things I wore, but she never said a word of criticism or advice, whether out of heroic tolerance or because she never noticed anything so unimportant as clothes, I do not know. She serenely let me make an ass of myself. It was Jas a little later who remarked cryptically, 'If you would only dress like a tart everyone would see you weren't one.'

At Somerville I was fortunate in being given a beautiful room in the new Maitland building, on the ground floor opening on to the garden. A room of my own was bliss to start with. I arranged it with care to my liking, with Islamic covers found in tin trunks of Father's in the ironing cellar at home, added bright silk cushions and hung a terracotta drawing done by Jas. I bought myself a 'Minty' wicker chair, copious as a small bed and of an elegant shape. They were the coveted thing, excellent and durable. Do they still exist?

The first evening was rather overwhelming. The whole college assembled outside the dining hall. It was the rule that senior students must always take in a junior. Some fourth year girl offered me her arm. Was this meant to be manly? It was always ritually done and we all crocodiled in. We addressed each other as Miss So-and-so. Among one's friends it was shortened to the surname only, as among men. Two by two we went in and took our places. For the first time my ears were affrighted by the violent treble vibrato of a hall full of intense females talking for dear life. I never got used to this detestable sound.

The second disagreeable impression was the earnestness that pervaded the place. I was two years older than the other newcomers who were straight from school and seemed to me like silly pretentious school-girls. Those of my age, the third year students, were already lined, haggard and spotty, terri-fied of their approaching finals and the possible collapse of all their earnest hopes. They all looked ready for a breakdown. The fourth year were more stable but had almost ceased to be human.

Of the girls in my year the most unhappily earnest by far was Miss Ellis Fermor, later to become Principal of the college. She was less lucky than I, having an ugly room in the old part, ill-lit and furnished with what might be described as discarded brown. In this she sat, nervously tensed up. On the other hand, in the room next to mine was a girl whose chief interest was the personal aura. She believed hers to be blue. She therefore covered her room with blue chintz and fitted blue bulbs into her electric lamps. On entering one swam into a sort of cobalt tank. I could not stand it. My aura must be orange. She later became a gossip writer. We all gave each other tea parties. One of the fourth year students gave such special teas she must surely have become a political or diplomatic hostess.

I had decided my Lancashire accent was perhaps not an adornment, so did my best to control my a's into ah's, with the result that at the end of a week it was known that I was Spanish and it was thought that under the circumstances my English was good. I soon learned from my first friend that there was more to a North Country accent than the a's. She pointed out that I clipped all my vowels, as mi book, th' door, etc. So I gave up trying. Twenty-five years later when I was living in Austria I discovered that Lancashire had filtered through even into my German—that the hitherto permissible short a's of man and can must now be mahn and kahn.

There was a sprinkling of black male students in Oxford, but few whites except foreigners, medical students and the unfit. All the rest had joined up, a whole generation. When my brother Phil, just out of hospital after an operation, came to visit me and we were walking across the college grounds, the Principal, Miss Penrose, was seen approaching. She was a tall Carnival figure, that is to say she looked as if her head and shoulders were being held up on a pole which tilted forward. She stopped as she was passing us. I introduced my brother and she replied, 'Young man, why are you not in uniform?' and moved on. That finished her for me. In any case I had no intention of keeping any of the protective rules. We were supposed to go about outside the gates in twos and threes, the years to add up to four. I preferred being alone and ran round Oxford as I had done Paris, loving every stone. I went to Evensong in Christ Church or New College nearly every day. If you can imagine Oxford when it was still the university and hardly yet a town, without car traffic and without the seething life of its young men, it was indeed as miraculously quiet as a noble dream.

I was doing classics and quickly learned how badly I had been taught and that I should never pass the first exam, but I still loved Greek and with it the shrewd humorous Scottish don who tutored me. If we had that vicious creature a MAN to tea in our rooms we had to ask a don to come and chaperone us. When Harold, in uniform, came my tutor was the one I shamefacedly asked. It seemed too tiresome for a don to have to do this. She came willingly and was very charming, but afterwards I spared her and simply let him in through the window. He had joined the Suffolk Regiment and was in training in Cambridge, only paying me a short visit.

I had not been in College two days before I was called upon by a member of the Oxford Christian Union, counterpart of what I knew in Cambridge as the Kickyou. A young woman whose type I knew all too well desired to know if I was saved. I had had too much of being saved and my religion now had an opposite orientation. In the happiness of my own room I was reading Spinoza, though I could not accept determinism.

Next Margaret Murray, a great charmer, tried to make me a social reformer. This was earnestness to the nth and in the full swing of modernity, but it seemed to me that all this earnestness was second best, it was incompatible with the shock, the bombardment of new sensations and the emotional vistas of merely being. Then there was the war. It had not yet shown what it was to become, and was still expected to be short, but it knocked the earnestness out of exams, or so it seemed to me, since I did not guess that after the war seven women out of every eight would have to earn their own living.

The violation of Belgium was the propaganda used to rouse idealists. The city of Oxford was to receive a train load of refugees. Some organiser of the proper-thing-to-do decided that Somerville College should greet them at the station with their national anthem. We were all drilled in this and learned the words, which in our pronunciation could only have underlined their feeling of exile. The gesture passed unacknowledged by the wretched arrivals and it was all we ever had to do with them.

*

The Christmas holiday was nightmarish. The top floor of our house had been requisitioned for billeting troops. Frances and I cooked mountains of bacon for their breakfast but otherwise saw nothing of them and they were quiet and orderly. The streets of Southport were full of marching men, the air re-echoed with their tramping. The Lancashire Regiment seemed made up of identical, rickety near-dwarfs, all showing off and as to tough they were stunted. I could not believe my eyes. Were these the average men of my proud county? Where did they come form—the cotton mills or the mines? It was pathetic and horrifying, and also impressive.

Nowadays at least there is no physical difference between richer and poorer, but I had no doubt that these were grinning ferocious fighters. Their jokes as they tramped past me in the street were frightening, aimed at me.

At home Mother was in only just contained hysterical despair. She believed, as did I, every word of propaganda about the holiness of the war. Jas, who in Cambridge had become a close friend of C. K. Ogden, was sceptical and derisive, firmly believing that the war was a fraud and had nothing to do with him. He had just returned from the studio in Munich and saw nothing wrong with the Germans. The chief objects of his bitter humour were the British fathers who 'gave their sons'. I thought this callous and stupid of him, since 'gave' only meant accepted that they must lose, and that is clearly a terrible grief. However, there was Jas at home making us all laugh. I remember when the boat carrying Kitchener was sunk and he went off first, Jas's rendering of the scene was so outrageously funny that Mother ran out of the room weeping. Frank was finishing his medical course at Cambridge which absolved him from joining up, but Jas, her eldest and most promising son, was refusing to serve his country. She was like a Roman matron and suffered corroding humiliation.

*

During my second term at Somerville I grew increasingly restless. The Trojan War? I wanted to be sharing the experience of my generation. I was now twenty-one and had come into my money, a totally free agent. I often heard the other girls complaining that their parents would not allow them to travel or to study something as unremunerative as Art or in any way to follow their own inclinations. I seriously suggested an Anti-Parents Society and offered to finance my friends. They were intensely shocked. They could not possibly displease their parents, and in our generation it was unthinkable to receive money. I had only offended them.

I decided to leave college and go to the war as a nurse. The

Bursar had French connections and promised to try to find me a place in a French hospital. Meanwhile a relative who had been a Sister at St Thomas's hospital arranged for me to go there for two months as a free-lance V.A.D. Frances was working in a hospital in Southport; her job was cleaning the lavatories. Heroic, but I aimed at France where it was all going on.

St Thomas's was a major experience. I thought it superb. It ran like a perfectly adjusted machine. The high standards, the practical routine, the ritual style and hierarchy of authority, the total devotion and medical skill delighted me. This was something really good. It was entirely supported by charity and independent. The National Health Service was not yet thought of.

I was in a surgical ward for men, not the war-wounded, but traffic accidents and major operations. My jobs of course were unskilled, but I could watch and we were taught by the Sister. I absorbed all I could, like taking deep breaths.

I lived in lodgings by the Marble Arch and crossed London by bus morning and evening. I knew nobody in London except a friend of Jas who had stayed with us at home. As it happened he was in the same lodging, but all the time I was there he never spoke to me. I felt it inexplicable and cruel. I was, outside the hospital, so lonely that it hurt. Sundays were a misery. I went long bus rides in every direction to learn my way about London, or took trips on the river steamers. I was pursued by hateful men if I dawdled. Harold sometimes promised to come and I waited all day in vain. Once he explained casually that he had been out with another girl. He told me about his lady loves as naturally as my brothers did.

Consequently all my interest was in the hospital. Any free time I had in the week I spent in the gallery of the operating theatre, watching with interest and some nausea what went on there. The nausea was cancelled out by the unexpected beauty of the scene, the mirror quality of all the shining machines and equipment, and the composition formed by the

(97)

circle of white-clad and veiled assistants, each dependent on a junior to hand or take, all grouped round the central figure of the surgeon, and the light focused on one small, bare patch of the shrouded body. It was a Giotto to watch. I also appreciated the clown's humour of the lowest in the hierarchy who after the operation cleared away the legs and other discards. No emotional quick change could be more theatrical.

Otherwise from sheer loneliness I had to live for my patients. There was among them a very decent elderly man who could not sleep for worrying about three little girls that he had left alone at home. I went off in the evening to visit them in the East End, taking sweets and toys. The eldest was eleven. She was a capable little thing, well able to look after her sisters. She got the little ones out of bed and they were all delighted to get a message from their father. I stayed with them perhaps an hour and then went back to St Thomas's. My ward was now under the night Sister who did not know me, but took me for a relative. The anxious patient, having had reassuring news, with love and kisses from his pretty ones, settled down to sleep and I went back to my lodgings.

Another patient was a young policeman, a Highlander whose speech I could hardly understand. I washed his splendid neck and shoulders every day with pleasure. There were no snags here such as a beard or bald head. I never knew whether to wash a bald patch. It seemed a little officious. My Highlander, coming from so great a distance, never had a visitor. It occurred to me that it would relieve both his boredom and mine if I acted the part. On Sunday afternoon I dressed up in my all too eccentric summer best and laden with grapes and flowers sailed into the ward. I made my way through the crowd of visitors to the one unvisited. It was a calamity. The Sister pounced on me like a hawk on a sparrow and hustled me outside where she lectured me with a rage like snapping shears. No nurse must ever visit a patient except on duty, still less ever show friendship for any particular one. She was there to attend to an injury, not to a person. What I had done was the unpardonable thing.

No one had told me of this rule, but perhaps a more modest girl would have invented it for herself.

I was removed from the men's surgical and put in the women's medical. It was a dreary change. Here there was no drama, no laughter. An underling like me was never told what any listless patient was suffering from. In a surgical ward the mood is of recovery, in the medical it was of lingering and despair. However, the two months allowed me for training were nearly up, after which I returned home to await a call to France.

Meanwhile I went every day to Liverpool to the out patients' department and there learned that St Thomas's was an ideal not reached in the provinces. The doctor in charge of out patients was a brute. He was surrounded by medical students, and the patients were brought in like animals for the students' practice, not for their own benefit. I remember a modest and frightened young woman being forced to have her body fumbled and pressed by all the students, to harden their embarrassment, never mind hers. Perhaps students have to learn to be inhuman in order to survive the stress. I had to see a reluctant student make his first unsure incision in the groin of a six-month-old baby, unanaesthetised. There was nothing for me to do but look on, and I felt I was being shown how everything shouldn't be done, not how it should, besides being shocked and made to feel sick every day by the doctor's behaviour.

I quickly removed myself from the Liverpool hospital and resorted to Cambridge, where Frank was at St John's, Phil at King's doing music, Harold in camp and Jas in lodgings on King's Parade where I joined him.

The war was growing in deadliness and was the undercurrent of all thought. Nevertheless, or even because of it, this period of my life was intensely happy. I had the company of the four people with whom I was most at home, a closed circle. With my brothers I was at all times, dressed or naked, entirely at ease. The difference of bodily formation seemed to make no difference to thought, feeling or reaction. All was clear and open between us. We were of the same kind. This gave me a simple attitude towards men that later caused continual mistakes. I thought they were natural friends.

Our landlady, Mrs Palmer, was a motherly woman never out of temper with us. She cooked all our meals and carried them up from the basement to the first floor. She did her very best for us, but it was not always appreciated. One 'special' pudding made for some occasion was found uneatable. We recklessly threw it out of the window on to King's Parade, not having the wit to realise till it was sailing through the air, that it would be very conspicuous. In the early morning as I looked out of my window to see how much it showed, I saw the policeman on his beat unselfconsciously carrying away some of our pudding on the toe of his boot. We thought this blissfully funny. Our silliness was not the high spirits of intoxication. Our whole family on both sides was teetotal. I had not yet tasted wine or spirits, but Harold in the army was learning fast, and Jas had lived in the Quartier Latin. Nevertheless no wine had reached our table.

It was summer. I spent my days on the river which I had almost to myself. Cambridge was empty during the day but crowded with young officers in the evening. The old Red Lion was like an officers' club. Its ancient waiter, Plum, with warm civility and aching feet did his best to serve the milling and voracious crowd. I dined there once or twice with Harold, but felt like a cat among a hundred dogs. Harold had made friends among the officers of whom he talked constantly. His life as a workman in the tannery had brought him in company with no one of his own kind. Now among his equals he was expanding with joyful excitement, surprised that the world had such goodly people in it. He made friends never to be forgotten. He introduced none of them to me. They all roared about on motor bikes, and Harold, now enjoying officer's pay, bought himself the latest model. It was then that he gave me his cast off two stroke. When Nora Hughes, a friend from Somerville, came to stay with us on a visit, I doubled the hazards of my driving by taking her on my carrier. I wonder that either of us survived.

Harold found time to take me on his carrier now and again. We went careering off on a very different highpowered flight to all his favourite woods and hills. There we sat among haystooks in the moonlight and looked out at the wide view and listened to the owls, but never touched each other even though the stars came out over us.

I lived in fact much like a swallow or a bat, enjoying river and sky and space and buildings, and finding that more than enough; but I also went every evening to Evensong in King's College Chapel, then as yet unembellished and overwhelmingly beautiful. The sound of the King's bell at 5.15 calling us in is still to me the most evocative sound I know, bracketed perhaps with that of a mountain stream tumbling over stones, the one Christian, the other pagan, one going in and in, the other spreading out and out.

Jas in Cambridge had always been very good to me, inviting me when he was an undergraduate to come for all the special musical events, the first production of Handel's *Semele* by Dr Rootham, *The Magic Flute*, the B minor Mass in King's which was an awakening of explosive importance. He also told me what was currently important to read or see. He now spent most of his time with C. K. Ogden, whose rooms were above the fishy smell in Petty Cury. With I. A. Richards they made a close trio. Jas, unlike Harold, would always introduce me to his friends. He took me into Ogden's sanctum but I was unimpressed. He may have had a brain whirring like a computer, but in himself struck me as a silly old woman with no values but giggles. Many years later when I had become interested in palmistry, being eager to see how these famous brains would be shown, I asked him to show me his hands. They were soft and white and had *no lines at all.* I have only seen this astonishing phenomenon once since, and that was on the hands of a girl living on her beauty, having and needing nothing else whatsoever. Perhaps Ogden had nothing but his computer.

*

There was always a room for Harold in our lodgings and there were nights when he did not have to sleep in camp. On one such night—I do not remember at all what preceded it—I woke up to see him in my room. I would not have been startled by this, except that he was more real than reality. Perhaps that is the special quality of hallucinations and explains why they are so obsessive. If this was a hallucination it is the only one I ever had. I saw that he was not there. To investigate the phenomenon I left my bed and went up to his room. I slipped into his bed as naturally as I would have joined him in a punt.

'Were you in my room just now?'

'No, I was here.'

'Funny, I saw you there.' He received me without surprise, embarrassment or misunderstanding. I was virgin as Shakespeare's heroines are, as were his own three sisters, but when I felt the length of his body against mine and the thudding of his heart under my head, it was something I hadn't bargained for at all. I isolated the shock of it from my behavioural consciousness, retarding it for future evaluation. We spent an amicable night without the hint of a caress, but without sleep. It was rather like being in a rowing boat following a spring tidal wave at Arnside, confident but aware of the cosmic force we were riding.

In the morning Mrs Palmer came in with the daily tin saucer bath and water cans that she carried to each room. Cambridge lodgings did not run to baths and in 1977 when I was house hunting for a friend I was amused to find how many well-built, well-proportioned houses still had no more than a loo in the garden. On this morning Mrs Palmer, having placed the bath and cans on the floor, turned to the bed.

'So that's where you are, Miss Lucy,' she said, surprised but not upset. I just grinned at her, thinking, 'This is better than Mother'. I was less pleased when her old husband popped up from the basement as I went out and leering called up, 'So Mr Boston's a lucky man!'

Twenty years later when I returned to Cambridge from abroad, an old woman caught my arm in the street. 'Miss Lucy, don't you remember me? Mrs Palmer.' I greeted her warmly, being at that time almost friendless. She went on—'I've so often wondered about you. Did you marry Mr Boston?'

'Yes, I did. But he has left me.'

'Oh, Miss Lucy! How you did love that boy!' (What a voice from the past.)

*

My adventure into nonconformity I celebrated with a short poem. I showed it to Jas from whom I had no secrets nor he from me. I know he had done the same with a chorus girl whose beauty in a photograph seemed to me almost unbelievable. Young people brought up as closely as we were, with no contacts outside their own family, are liable when they find themselves in the unexpected world to launch off in gauche and idiotic courses. Jas's chorus girl, he told me, was taking to drink, and he was trying to cure her. Did he think .that by showing her that he respected her, he would coax her to keep off drink? It seemed to me that if she loved him, as she surely did, his cure was likely to make her worse. I did not consider myself in love with Harold, but I had grieved sympathy with Jas's girl.

It was no doubt with the intention of pleasing me that a week later Jas showed me the *Cambridge Review* with my simple and explicit poem printed in it, and another of even less value. I was outraged and told him so, after which to revenge himself on my ingratitude, the two poems, which he had arbitrarily caused to be printed, were referred to as Lucy's bilious attacks. That put a stop to my poetry for fifteen years.

Throughout the summer while the war grew ever less imaginable, I stayed on in Cambridge. I took to sleeping out in a punt up by Byron's pool, where Harold could slip out of camp and join me for an hour or two. Once waking up alone in the dawn I saw a kingfisher perched on my wrist, a portent surely. Or, I went by canoe along the rapidly diminishing upper river until even a canoe could be forced no further. Canoes are not good for sleeping in, but if they are well mud-grounded it is possible. Coming back into Cambridge in the early morning still full of wonder, I was amused to hear an early riser on the bank say to his companion, 'Gawd! She's come from the mountains!'

However, I had not forgotten that I meant to nurse. As I still heard nothing from the Bursar at Somerville about an opening in France, I signed on at the old Addenbrooke's Hospital for the time being. It was hard after the boundless freedom I had been enjoying. I had to move to the nurses' lodging where I shared a room with a good-tempered V.A.D. She had a sober steady disposition and thick black hair down to her ankles. What a weight and responsibility to carry on your head in the ward! I was fascinated to watch her disposing the long rope-like bands in such a way that a nurse's starched cap could be perched on top. She accepted me very tolerantly.

I was to begin on night duty. There was a very attractive Sister over me, who was having a happy time with the doctor on night duty. She told me, as if out of pure kindness, to go off, to go to sleep, or read. Or perhaps do a little polishing, perhaps the candlestick and inkstand. She would call me if she needed me. I had nothing to do until the 5 a.m. washing and bed making. Every night was wasted and this was the only time I could see Harold. I was allowed out in the afternoon and used to go and sit disconsolate in the sitting room in King's Parade, where Mrs Palmer lovingly cosseted me and listened to my laments.

Jas

Phil

Phil

Harold

Luckily after a month I was changed to day duty in a ward full of old women and teenagers.

There was a pretty girl with severe St Vitus' dance; she might really have been possessed of the devil. She was kept curtained off from the ward because any movement set her off. She twisted and sprang in her bed like a newly caught fish in the bottom of a boat. Her contortions were frequently violent enough to fling her out of bed. We were forever picking her up off the floor. Her midday meal was always and only kidney beans which I had to administer as best I could to the involuntarily side-stepping mouth. Sedatives if they were invented had not yet reached Cambridge. Again St Thomas's put the provincial hospital to shame. All the red tape was here, but it had become obstructive and lost significance. I liked nursing and still thought the patients were the important part, but the ward Sister was sour and hostile. If a sheet was caught on a wire of the bedstead, she would deliberately rip it in half in order to blame me. It shocked me very much to have to scrub out the bed pans in the bath used by the patients. Also, instead of curtains that could be pulled to screen patients when necessary, the nurses had to carry three heavy bamboo screens the length of the ward and back. My feet cried to high heaven for relief.

After work we had to return to our lodging and stay there. It was not long before the landlady came to tell me there was someone to speak to me at the door. It was Harold of course.

'Ho! It's you. I *am* glad. Come up to my room.'

The landlady interposed her rigid body. 'Certainly NOT,' she said.

'Why not? This is my cousin. We must sit somewhere and there's nowhere else.'

'No visitors are allowed in the nurses' rooms. Certainly not *men.*'

She made the word sound very dirty. We both burst into laughter. 'Oh well, we'll just sit on the stairs.'

So we sat on the stairs and made great merriment for an

hour or so, the landlady's grim face appearing from below every now and then, hoping to see worse than she did. We made an appointment for Sunday afternoon when I was free, and then I let him out.

When the happy day came I discarded the starched cap and knife-edged belt and put on what were then called 'gladrags', probably, and most unsuitably, a dress of apricot silk. We mounted the motor bike, and clutching my young officer round the waist I waved derisively at Addenbrooke's as we roared past along the Trumpington Road.

On the Monday I was summoned to the Matron's room where my sins were enumerated before me. She had seen me wearing a ring when on duty in the ward. (It was a small signet ring inherited from my father. I looked on it as part of my hand. Even St Thomas's had not objected.) Secondly I powdered my face. Who could have guessed, untold, that these were sins? Thirdly, my landlady complained of my trying to introduce men into my bedroom and of improper behaviour on the stairs. And lastly, I had been seen riding through the town on the carrier of an officer's motor cycle. Unfitting conduct for a decent girl. I was dismissed.

I was too contemptuous to be hurt. I finished my day in the ward, said goodbye to my patients and was warmed by the regrets of the old women whom I left behind uncherished in their beds.

I returned bouncing with release to Jas and Phil. I wrote to Mother telling her casually that I had been dismissed, and thought no more about it. She of course, as I should have known, took it as total disgrace reflecting on the whole family. Little as she thought of my morals, she travelled down instantly to Cambridge and went to see the Matron in my defence, a painful act of loyalty. I cannot imagine the scene, but Mother's quiet manners and grief, even perhaps her tears, had overcome the starch of the Matron. After all, they really saw eye to eye. Mother returned to us triumphant, to announce that the Matron would take me back.

Nothing was further from my intention. Of course I was not going back. I had had no idea Mother was cherishing any such hope in her mind. I thought she was just clearing the family name. I hope I thanked and was kind to her, but I don't remember feeling anything but offhand. I was not going to be managed by Mother or the Matron, both of whom had ideas of behaviour that I found insulting. Mother saw that there was nothing to be done with me. She travelled home the next day and I did not even go with her.

*

Soon afterwards the Suffolk Regiment was to be moved further south. Harold came to say goodbye to us. His behaviour was odd. Every few minutes he made sentimental lurches toward me with 'I say, Lucy—' which never got any further. It was a little time before I realised he was drunk, and I might never have understood if Phil had not been choking with laughter. He had not seen one of his family in this plight before. It certainly makes for domestic hilarity. This was the last time I ever saw Phil. I was pleased with even drunken advances from Harold, never having had any sober ones.

The next day I went home to Southport, but I had no sooner got there than Harold's sister rang up to tell me he had had a bad road accident on his motor bike and was in hospital. The Suffolk Regiment had gone off without him. I went to the Bostons' house to get more details. He had crashed on the Newmarket road, had broken a knee, crushed a hand and a foot, and had concussion. How bad was he? Nobody knew. His father, that very silly man, was pacing round the house puffing out his cheeks and blowing his moustache upwards, in gusts of self pity.

'I am the most unfortunate of men. I have no luck. Fate crushes me again and again. Here's my eldest son, nothing much to be proud of perhaps but still my eldest, and he's a cripple, good for nothing. A miserable cripple good for nothing at all.'

Fury filled me. I took the first train back to Cambridge.

The military hospital was set up in the fields behind Queen's Road. I had to get permission to visit from the officer in charge. I was embarrassed, having understood by now that my appearance was not reassuring. The Colonel looked me up and down and turned away to suppress his amusement. He gave generous permission.

I found Harold in a private room, a small wooden cell. He was in great pain and, in the excitement that follows shock, wound up, noisy and difficult, but also desperately funny and taking it all with high spirits. His elderly nurse already doted on him. A face screwed up in equal degrees of pain and laughter is irresistible.

*

Autumn was upon us. Each enclosing evening, a time when the smell of fallen leaves increases, I walked to the hospital across Garret Hostel Bridge, then a slender iron span. The Backs, with double avenues of vast elms and deep shadowy spaces, were unlit and empty. Cambridge was soundless except for the college bells ringing for Evensong. I walked in full consciousness of what closed me round or opened above me, awed to be so small, moving among so much.

Harold had no other visitor. His dear friends in the regiment had all gone, his sisters were unable to come, Phil was already away at a Flying School. Jas perhaps was just leaving it to me. I was well received. The devoted nurse accepted me with kindness. Harold lay with one leg attached to an extension, the foot considered irreparable done up in plaster, his right hand strapped out on a wide splint. He was helpless, but a spluttering jet of passionate humour. I went regularly for every possible minute, taking anything I thought might relieve him. I chose a Medici reproduction of Velasquez's Captain Bartolomeus Borro to break the enclosing monotony of his wooden walls, a boisterous portrait that could make one laugh. Once sitting at the head of his bed I had constituted myself as his prop and bedrest. I was wearing a rose red silk blouse on which his head rested. This was the evening chosen by the Matron for an inspection. Rattling with starch and pendant accoutrements, scissors, pens, note book, keys, she appeared in the doorway flanked by her underlings. She gave me glowering looks and withdrew under my grin. It was the woman who had dismissed me from Addenbrooke's. I daresay the aiding and abetting nurse was scolded, but perhaps officers were allowed visitors from the demi-monde. Who else would they know, so far from home?

In time, Harold was on crutches, one of his very personal and dynamic hands deformed but fully usable, his foot lacking several bones still in plaster. The surgeon had told him he would never walk again.

I think we must both have gone home for Christmas, but the next thing that I remember is that Jas, Harold, Nora Hughes and I were up at Llyn Ogwen, at what was then Mrs Jones's cottage. Here I met for the first time I. A. Richards of whom I had heard so much from Jas. He was standing outside the cottage, obviously not expecting us. I got the impression of a very unfriendly man, embarrassed, moving himself whenever we moved so as always to face us squarely, as if on the defensive. He edged nearer and nearer to the cottage till he could back into it. I admit I was very disappointed. However, a little while later he came out again all friendly and at peace, but now with a very large patch of sacking tacked, probably by Mrs Jones, over the seat of his trousers. Next day he began to initiate me into simple short climbs over nearby boulders and a small chimney, in which Harold, to disprove the surgeon, joined us, discarding his crutches. That heavily plastered foot was dragged up through the snow after its fellow and one and a half clinging hands. No mention of that foot was ever allowed again. He forced it to do everything he wished, though I think every limping step hurt to the end of his life. However on this occasion to my relief, having proved his point, he climbed no more, but crutched along the valley with Jas instead. Jas had brought

(109)

into the wilds of Wales a crate of claret and after supper we all got very convivial. I drank too much and disliked it.

We must have returned to Ogwen in the spring, taking Nora Hughes with us. Ivor was there again and he took Nora and me slab climbing. I was more agile and quick than she, but I could never look downward or outward, so that while she was fumbling in her agonisingly slow way I had to stand on my ledge with my eyes shut. After she had left I spent some days scrambling about with Ivor, but could not enjoy descending the steps of a small waterfall sitting in the water. Later Jas told me Ivor had said I was uncivilised. I recognised this as true and was much discouraged.

It was at Ogwen that Harold had the greatest sorrow of his life, the death in the trenches of his friend Ian Claughton. This grief he never lost.

6

Early in 1916 I got my offer of work in a French military hospital, so long waited for. I collected the outfit recommended, fortunately not so miserably starched and Victorian as for English wards, but comfortable white overalls and a large square of lawn to cover the hair, perfectly natural and rather becoming. Mother urged me to buy pyjamas instead of nightgowns because they would be better for escaping from pursuing Germans. In fact throughout the war I never saw a German.

Before setting off I spent the last evening with Harold in London, probably at the Alhambra, a fake-Scheherazade shrine of romance that entirely filled my needs. Few people with less than my age will now remember that beautiful and to me mysterious haunt of youth and high spirits, balcony above balcony all with Moorish arches, the whole vast crimson space excellently proportioned and softly lit. I hope if I could go back to it now I should not find it tawdry and vulgar. It remains in memory as an enchantment in the middle of London.

We must on this occasion have missed my train, for I remember us bundling into a taxi with much laughter and saying casually to the driver, 'Take us to Southampton.'

'Yessir. Southampton Row.'

'No. Southampton.'

'Yessir. Southampton.' He slammed the door and off we went.

I was wearing a very saucy hat with a veil drawn tight under my chin, perhaps chosen for travelling. Somewhere between Leicester Square and Southampton docks Harold broke into the conversation with 'For Christ's sake take off that bloody veil', and I received a first kiss, possibly his very first, for it was abrupt and of the hit or miss variety, hopelessly inexpert. I was grateful for the intention and we may even have completed the journey arm in arm. I am quite sure we had not got as far as hand in hand.

I went on to the boat alone, seeing no other passenger. Perhaps they were already in their berths. I stood a long time on the deck looking at the great pool with its circle of reflected lights. Beside our steamer there were only a few smaller boats, their masts very slightly swaying against the sky. It was a still, dark night. No sound came from the open water outside, but the call of the oceans brooded insistently. No one could have told there was a deadly war being fought across the Channel. There were no searchlights, no blackout, no convoys, no aeroplanes overhead. It was a Channel crossing like any other, nor did this strike me as strange, having no prophetic foresight.

*

I spent the next day wandering round Le Havre by myself, then crossed the rough mouth of the Seine in a tossing cockleshell of a boat to the Normandy coast and finally arrived at my destination, Houlgate, late at night. I reported at the bureau and an orderly showed me to my room, which was large and luxurious. The volunteer nurses were housed in one of the best hotels in the resort, all of which had been commandeered by the army. I opened the tall french windows and could hear the sea rolling gently on a beach close below me.

My luggage had gone astray. I did not wish to sleep in the underclothes I had already worn for two days of travel, so, still Scheherazading, I shawled my naked self in a yard-wide red chiffon scarf I had worn round my neck. It was delicious on the skin, light and warm. I slept serenely.

What I had not expected was a knock on the door next morning and the irruption, before I was quite awake, of four other English nurses come to welcome me, with coffee and croissants. They were taken aback at the sight of their new acquisition lying there so voluptuously in a spread of dark hair and all too transparent crimson chiffon. One, a genteelly reared Surrey girl, burst into laughter and thereafter became a friend. Another, by far the vulgarest woman I ever knew, withdrew muttering. She was a trained nurse, probably dismissed from her hospital, though it is not for me to say so. The third was an elderly Scottish nurse, very trustworthy, and the last the daughter of a bishop, educated and charming and correct, but like me untrained. All were living in the same hotel. Downstairs were wards large and small. The view from my window along the coast was splendid, and the nearest building was the Casino, also a hospital.

My luggage arrived after breakfast, so I was able to dress and report for duty. The office was a small room in the Casino, presided over by a fatherly but very gross sergeant and a slightly lame young aristocratic assistant whose lands were a few miles inland. I became in time fond of both of them. They were a standby in a world turned upside down.

I must explain that French military hospitals, if this one was a fair example, did not consider nurses necessary. There was in France no profession of nursing, only nuns. There were orderlies, rough untrained types who dealt with the bed pans and took round the meals, served in the tin cans of the trenches. No beds were remade once the patients were in them. Nobody bedridden was washed. No rooms were cleaned, no charts were kept over the beds. The dressings of all mobile patients were done in the *Salle de Pansements*, and here voluntary French ladies came to help. There was no one on duty at night except officially the orderlies who, as they worked all day, were naturally sound asleep. There had originally been volunteer nurses at night, but as they were too often found in bed with the patients in the morning, night nursing had been forbidden. The nurse whose place I had taken, had, in sweeping out a ward that offended her, found under a bed a kit bag containing a German's head. All these horrors were told me over *déjeuner* the first day.

The English nurses had taken over the wards as a matter of course and were carrying on according to their English lights, two of them actually rustling in starch. Their officiousness must have caused some surprise, but they were considered harmless by the indifferent authorities and appreciated by the patients. There was nobody over us, no one to whom we were responsible. We were simply allowed in.

I was appointed as assistant to an American lady who had a small ward of her own adjoining the operating theatre. She was a gaunt woman of sixty or so, with the face of a bothered sheep. She had all the generosity and idealism of Americans but no sense at all. She had given untold money to buy equipment for the hospital theatre, and so was well in with the *Médecin-Chef*, himself a totally insignificant, trim toy soldier. The theatre was not used for big operations in this type of hospital, but it was used. It was served by a middle-aged, evil-looking woman under the protection of the *Médecin-Chef*. She had the wide open empty blue eyes of one who uses speech only for lying.

The American lady presided over her ward of six beds, for slight operation cases. I would not be surprised if a few incisions had been made to keep her happy. She was fussy, muddle-headed and self-important. She had come over to make a difference to the war. Her French was of the kind one hears assayed in Paris shops.

Predictably she disliked me at sight. Her patients did not go to the *Salle de Pansements* but their wounds were dressed and bandaged by her. It happened that I was a good bandager. I had taken the trouble to acquire this neat and amusing art. Later on in my nursing days when there was much ragging of a patient, '*Sans Fesses*', who had lost his buttocks, I was the only person in the hospital who could criss-cross him

(114)

comfortably in such a way that it would not drop off. But now I was merely an assistant. The American Nightingale was unhandy. She could not get the hang of this business of changing the roll from one hand to the other as you circled the shoulder or waist of a standing man. She *walked* round him, nearly always dropping the bandage before she got back to the starting point so that it rolled away across the ward floor. As I retrieved it, perhaps from under a bed, and began the slow process of rolling it up again to replace in her hand, watched by the boys with lovely grins, it was difficult to remain solemn and not to act it as a comedy. Why in fact should one be solemn? I did control myself, but she sensed a lack of respect.

The function of this hospital was to take from the casualty clearing station those men not too seriously wounded to be moved. It was for *soldats* only. The officers presumably were better treated. The men came in train loads, filled up two hotels and the Casino and remained a few weeks, till they were all moved on and the place was got ready for the next batch. When I got there, the majority of the patients were on their way to recovery. Those who could walk were free to go out and get drunk with their friends in the bistro. It was considered a sure way to make your sepsis active again. One of my six men was still bedridden. Alone in the ward when his mates were out, he was bored and homesick. I acquired a draughts board and sat on the side of his bed to play with him. The American Nightingale coming in unexpectedly in the evening shrieked at me.

'Nurse! Get off that bed at once! Don't you know it's unprofessional to sit on a patient's bed?' I could have said it was unprofessional to roll surgical bandages across a dirty floor, but I said mildly, 'We were only playing draughts'.

'Never do such a thing again. I feel I hardly dare leave the ward.'

I left the ward in a rage and almost bumped into the arms of the anaesthetist, who considered a kiss but thought better of it. He was an excellent, well brought up young man. We had a long amused conversation and I forgot the insult I had received.

Next morning I heard that the American Nightingale had seen the *Médecin-Chef* and asked to have me sent home. Dismissed again, and so soon! Luckily for me the *Médecin-Chef* had an eye for laughing girls and couldn't bring himself to do it. With a cynical wish to please all he sent me word instead to take over two upper floors of the biggest hotel, in all two hundred men. They were almost all up and about, but had to report each day to the *Salle de Pansements*, to which I now had entry. It was a large gilded room, one whole side of which was windows looking on to the sea, probably once the dining room. From the ceiling hung chandeliers enclosed in holland covers thick with dust.

There was a doctor in charge and four French ladies assisting. Half a dozen men at a time stood round stripping to show wounds in various parts of their anatomy. One of the French ladies was a mad, bitter creature who with her probe deliberately made each dressing as painful as possible, saying as she did it, 'My brother was killed in the trenches. Why weren't you? (Jab) I'll see to it there's no malingering here.'

Another had her sixteen-year-old daughter beside her, a slim, snow-white, baby-faced Botticelli Madonna in hospital overall and cap. Here was the '*jeune fille bien élevée*' that I so little resembled. She was so suppressed by upbringing she could neither risk a word nor a half smile, only modest, mute docility. Her mother kept a sharp lookout and if any male body was likely to be uncovered anywhere between the armpits and the knees, Mother tapped on the floor with her heel and the untainted maiden slipped out of the room. Heads, arms and feet only were polite enough.

The other two French women were duchesses with awe-inspiring historical names. At *déjeuner* they shared a table with the oddly assorted English, but did not mix with us. They did not expect us to understand French, and I was the only one who had any real grasp of it. They were talking about 'un pauvre blessé' whose state was so disgusting that it made them sick. They had had to abandon him. 'Le pauvre, c'est trop écoeurant'. I asked them then where he was, and learned he was in a single room somewhere in my two floors. I went in search, and presently found him. He was not young, a slight bottle-shouldered man with an undistinguished bald head and the eyes of a dog in a trap. He had lost all his lower jaw and much of the upper. He could neither speak nor eat. Such disfigurement cut him off from his fellows. He was in voluntary hiding—whenever I saw him, standing alone there in awful despair, unable to ask for anything, unable to think of his wife. I at least could dress his horrible wound, could see it and not reject him, could smile at him and bring him writing paper. There was no radio, no library, nothing day after day but silence and a view over the great empty sea and empty sky.

Before long he was moved off with all the rest, I hope to somewhere where faces are remade. It was beginning to be done. Soon after the war I met a man who was intriguingly handsome because his face gave no clue to his personality. It was a surgical face made for him after a disaster similar to that of my patient. From the latter I had a letter which pleased me very much. I had not been able to form any idea of what kind of man I was tending, his class or his intelligence, but his letter was written in a cultured hand, beautifully expressed and warm with thanks. He did not, alas, tell me what they were doing for him.

No doctor regularly visited my floors. Those needing dressings went down to him. Searching through the rooms I found others who needed attention. There was a man with a temperature of 104-105 whom I watched over at night in spite of the ruling but as nobody was looking after him, nobody knew. Considering how little training I had had, it was a wonder if I did not kill anybody by mistake. I did perhaps let one die by oversight. There was one room with

five ribald, lively men confined to bed for one reason or
another. Many Rabelaisian jokes were made about me, an
entertaining risk for them as they were never quite sure how
much *argot* I understood. I never minded what they said and
could take a pinch in the behind as nothing to worry about.
We were all young. In this larking ward there was a boy who
lay without joining in. He had an impassive face rather like
warm carved stone, a strong piece of sculpture. He left his
food untouched, but when I asked him if he was all right, if
he wanted anything, he looked away and would not answer.
He did not toss or cough, or show any sign of pain. I asked
the man in the next bed about him, but he just shrugged and
said, '*C'est le cafard*'. Certainly the memory of the trenches
was enough to leave one like that. However when the next day
he hardly seemed even to hear me, I reported him to the
doctor. He was found to have advanced double pneumonia.
Antibiotics were not yet invented so double pneumonia was
almost always fatal. The boy was moved to a sort of cupboard that might once have been the housemaid's closet,
which was where they now took patients to die. I feel sure
this boy was dying on purpose. He had sensed a way out. By
the time they had carried him to this secret hole he was as
good as dead.

The priest was brought, and the doctor stood by to register
a death. I knew nothing about Extreme Unction and was now
overwhelmed by the beauty and rightness of this send-off.
They then closed his hazel eyes, and I think he was dead. I
bent and kissed his forehead, thinking, 'I do this for his
mother', and at once was seized with fear that I had done yet
another unconsidered act, and perhaps cancelled out the
Unction. Nobody said anything. They had finished with him.

There were three priests on the staff. One, in charge of
food, was a gross bestial sinner who offered me his bed and
afterwards persecuted me with vile abuse. He was later dismissed for peculation and disorderly behaviour. Another was
a cultivated Jesuit, whose face struck me as enjoying a higher

(118)

form of wickedness, but I have nothing against him except the sanctimonious cuddling I referred to before. The third was young, thin, ill-favoured, bespectacled and deeply unhappy. He could look nobody in the eyes, perhaps because he could never be one with the hell-seasoned boys whom he served. I could not but respect him and it was he who administered Extreme Unction. I would have hated to offend him though I cared nothing for the opinion of the duchesses.

Now I had got the measure of it, nightly before I went off duty I went the rounds of two floors and said Goodnight to my one hundred and ninety-nine men.

Letters from home were as regular as in peacetime. They were stuck up on a board in what had been the entrance lounge of the hotel, now a sort of common room for the staff. Here on the green baize overlaced with diagonal white tapes I would find lodged letters from Mother, as if I were still at school, from Jas, now roped into an Officers' Training Camp, and if I was lucky, very funny pages from Harold.

*

As we were entirely voluntary and there was literally no one over us, we could have leave whenever it suited us. I must confess that as far as I remember, none of the other English nurses took any. I decided to go home for Christmas. I merely told the bureau when I was going. Frances was at home. She was having a gruelling time as a regular V.A.D. in the local hospital, not allowed any of the comi-tragic licence given to me. Mother was very proud of her. Harold was at his home, now able to wear two shoes and walk with a brisk but heavy limp. He had bought a small open car, in which after Christmas we set off together southward. We were overtaken by a heavy snowstorm. The car of course was unheated, the windscreen blocked with snow. To see out we had to open the windscreen and take the snow in our faces. There were as yet only carbide lamps, giving a poor light, and no roads had been improved to meet the future car traffic. The occasional car; a little less freakish than the very first, was not worth worrying about. So, no road clearance. We inched our way along narrow roads with only snow-heaped hedges to mark the way. At Huntingdon we could go no further. We put up at the old George Hotel, then pleasingly old-fashioned even to our eyes. Our bedroom had pictures of the Crimean War and a large iron bed, where our well-mannered intimacy was screwed up a turn tighter. I had almost a disease of honesty, and being unable to pass over the deceit of signing ourselves in the obligatory wartime visitors' book as Mr and Mrs, I confessed in the morning to the manageress that this was not so. She couldn't have been less interested. For a little thing like that she was not going to alter her visitors' list, war or no war.

Harold, impatient at being out of the war, had succeeded in being taken on as chauffeur to a specialist who toured the English military hospitals in France, so in future we would both be on the other side of the Channel though attached to different armies.

I went back to France alone. There were still no difficulties, formalities or precautions. One simply booked and walked on to the ship for Le Havre. A great many people were going backwards and forwards about their business, whatever that was. On this route there was no sign of the war.

There had been changes at Houlgate during my brief absence. The *Médecin-Chef* had been discharged for pocketing the money so liberally given by the American Nightingale for theatre equipment. She herself had left in indignant disillusionment. When I arrived the hospital was empty, waiting for a new train load. Meanwhile someone in the upper hierarchy of administration had decided that the wounded were to be classified according to the part of the body wounded. When the first lot arrived in the middle of the night there was pandemonium. They were all wounded in the feet. The hospital had only five pairs of crutches. No warning had been given. This lot did not stay long. It is to be hoped there were crutches where they were going, but if our hospital succeeded in laying in a supply, it was in vain, because the next lot were all eye cases. There was no eye specialist on our staff. Where both eyes were bandaged, the patients had to be fed, washed and guided about. There were not enough of us to feed them all and it is not a job one can do with brutal speed. These also were moved on fairly soon, to make way for hands and arms.

I was now in the main Salle of the Casino, a lovely place with a wide terrace over the sea. It held perhaps fifty beds. The old Scottish nurse was in charge. She looked grim but treated me as if she had been our family Nanny. She might have said, 'Miss Lucy is rather wild but she will grow out of it.' She knew her job and I served under her very willingly. We got on easily, perhaps because we both had Nonconformist backgrounds. The Casino was filled with the elaborate brass bedsteads that had furnished the hotels, with knobs large and small and loops and uprights like the sides of the Forth bridge. My Nanny had been taught that brass is to be polished, and to this she rigidly adhered. She bid me take all the lacquer off the fifty bedsteads and keep them polished. What a wartime job to come out from England to do! I did as I was told. It was better than slovenliness. The doctor for instance in charge of this ward made his occasional rounds in mid-morning unwashed and unshaved, wearing a long military overcoat beneath which pyjama trousers showed, and unbrushed shoes on bare feet. In St Thomas's he would surely have been struck down, if not by lightning from above, then by the ward Sister. He greeted neither patients nor nurses, asked no questions. He had a cigarette hanging from his lip and merely walked round and out again, perhaps signing his visit in a book. It is true that no one was seriously ill in the ward. Their wounds were dressed. The era of pills for everything had not dawned and nobody expected personal attention. Perhaps he was just a realist, uninterested in style.

Daily I laboured diligently from bed to bed, chatting meanwhile with the amused occupant. In Nanny's time all those rail knobs and balls twinkled and flashed like a myriad

Christmas tree decorations, or like the sun on the wrinkled surface of the sea outside. The new *Médecin-Chef* used to look in at the door occasionally to admire this English fantasy.

*

Spring revealed the beauty of the Normandy countryside. It was not dramatic. The cliffs were made of black mud constantly slipping down, not beautiful in themselves but giving a grand view of the sea from the top. In every cove along the coast there were hotels and little towns but they were confined to the edge of the sea. All behind was purely pastoral, a rolling endlessly varied panorama of half-timbered farm houses in fields full of wild flowers, of orchards and woods and open hillsides, unlimited and unbroken by anything we should now call a road. I had enough free time for walking to explore round about, and almost immediately found I loved it as if I had been born there. Perhaps some distant ancestor had bequeathed me some thin nerve of racial memory that stirred. The only other place where I have felt immediately rooted is my present home, also Norman.

At first my walks were troubled by vagabond children pursuing me with Anglo-phobic balls of mud and pebbles, but in time I made friends with them and instead they brought me stolen flowers. I suffered the loneliness of all young people who feel themselves to be freakish, and these small adherents were a comfort to me. The two I liked best were sister and brother aged nine and seven. They had no home but lived in a collapsed shed on the shore. Their mother was a fat, drunken syphilitic, lying on the bare ground. I used to bandage her legs with hospital equipment. She seemed unable to move about and I have no idea what she lived on. The children, unlike Italian children, did not beg. For a time I fed them with hospital left-overs but the brutal *curé* stopped that. I used then to take five or six children out with me in the early morning to farms where meals could be provided. Along the cliff top, the farmers' wives in peacetime provided exquisite food for wealthy visitors and now they thought this crazy Miss was a godsend in a dead season, vagabond children and all. There was a delectable place perhaps six miles away, run in great elegance by an ageing, painted actress for the most discriminating clients from Trouville. Here I had the nerve to take my ragged gang at an unearthly hour, knocking till the old person got out of bed. She always received me with ready courtesy and served us the best coffee, butter and croissants I have ever eaten, under striped sunshades on neatly raked gravel. Who would blame her if she overcharged? My ragamuffins, being French, knew what was good and I never had any trouble with their behaviour. The hospital food was wretched, but food in Normandy was copious and unrestricted, war or no war. In the end I got my little girl housed in a good farm, and the little boy in a Catholic charity school in Caen. As I left the little creature with a sour old monk, my heart suddenly smote me, but alas, not hard enough to make me snatch him back. I have blamed myself ever since for a piece of interfering ignorant cruelty. Poor little devil, never free again and parted from his sister. I have never done a worse thing.

The hospital *curé*, my enemy, made my concern for the children another opportunity for abusing me. He said to me of them, '*Ça, c'est de la viande*'. I will not translate it because confirmed Francophil though I am, I prefer to think this appalling brutality has never been said in English.

*

Small waifs were not my only company. The anaesthetist, Ary, who was outstandingly honourable in this limbo of irresponsibility, had become devoted to me. We spent a great deal of time together in the frequent periods when the hospital had been emptied. Having once declared himself and been refused, he never plagued me with his desires but did everything he could think of to please and amuse. I was wooed at table with snails, frogs and blackbirds, which failed to please. He took me to Paris with him to stay with his parents and so gave me my only experience of French family life, for which I am ever grateful. His mother found me less dreadful than she had expected. She had feared a harpy. It was amusing to be so much liked because I was clearly not going to marry her son. His father was enchanting, an exquisitely courteous old man with a beautiful face. For the rest of my life I never went through Paris without visiting them. My friendship with Ary was of course noticed and avidly followed by the hospital and the village. It was so open that it was for that very reason intriguing.

As the spring advanced my roving habits increased. When not on duty I could not keep indoors. Apart from the early morning walks with the children, I would often go off alone at night and sleep in the woods or on a haystack up on the cliffs. None of the English nurses shared my fancies, nor my love of the sea. From April 1st to October I swam daily. It was easy to undress in an empty storeroom in the Casino and run across the terrace and down into the wide blue sea. For some reason this shore seemed not to make rough waves. The sea lapped eternally. If I swam far out I would meet white butterflies purposefully crossing over from distant Le Havre, flying in wavering but direct lines close to the surface of the water. Sometimes Ary joined me, but never anyone else. On warm nights of full moon the sea was irresistible. I would slip out alone, having the whole coastline to myself. Both sea and sky were the cloudy blue of skimmed milk, and the water at night seemed to be as full of small fish as soda water is of bubbles. They swam in under the neck of my bathing costume (ample and decent in those days) in swarms and felt most peculiar. I had to strip off my costume and turn it inside out to release them. I think they were whitebait. This delicious freedom and solitude was in France, in the Great War, and only just beyond the war zone.

In Rouen a little further up the Seine, Harold's elder sister, my particular friend, was nursing in a British hospital under great hardship, sleeping in a tent overrun by rats. We for our part had nothing worse than bugs and fleas. Bugs went to the laundry in our clothes, and after being well beaten on a stone by the brook, which was the method of laundry still practised, they came back hungry in the same garment. Fleas were easier to dispose of, but one day, knowing I had killed my fleas overnight, I was still plagued by itching. I admonished myself not to be neurotic and even persuaded myself the agony of itch was imagination. That night on undressing, I killed eight fleas on my person.

I decided to go and visit my friend in Rouen. From the easy-going anarchy of the French hospital nothing seemed simpler. I bought a ticket and took the train, arriving at Rouen late at night. At the station the exit was barred by a cordon of British soldiers. Where, they asked, was my permit? Permit? What for? Rouen was a British base and no one was allowed in without a permit. But I *am* British! Where's your *passeporte*? As I wasn't leaving France I didn't bring it. To my amazement I was arrested and taken before a very grim Colonel. The stony severity never left his face, it might have been a court martial leading to execution. However he sized up my silly innocence and ordered my guards to escort me to 'the convent' for the night and have me put on the first train in the morning. Could I not even see my cousin? Out of the question. I was marched off.

We arrived at the convent in the dark and I left before dawn, so I never saw it. I do not know where it was or what it was called. The Mother Superior received me with the greatest kindness. By a sudden change I found myself an honoured guest. I was given a charming guest room and supper was brought me by a nun. She left the door open while she arranged the tray, and in the passage outside a surge of nuns with wide-winged starched caps catching on each other like cow's horns gazed at me in fascinated curiosity and even delight. A novelty had come in. I've seldom had such a welcome, though wordless. However, before it was light I was woken and hurried off, being entrusted this time not to a posse of soldiers, but to a sinister figure like a stage Satan in a flapping black cloak and slouch hat. Without the convent's sanction I would not have dared to pass him in the street by daylight. I followed his beckoning as he strode off through narrow alleys across the unlit city back to the station, where he merely pointed, and left me.

The train was packed with French soldiers going on leave from the trenches. I was the only woman in the train. I squeezed myself into a compartment where they were already falling asleep as if they had not slept for weeks. They were a grievous sight, haggard wrecks of men hardly expecting to be alive. Many of them were having nightmares, shouting out or groaning. Before very long I had a heavy, unconscious head on each shoulder and another on my knees. I felt motherly and had an arm round the shoulders of one to keep him from slipping. My hand thus came into the keeping of an older man who could not get to sleep. He had a good face and why should he not hold my hand for comfort? I dozed, and when I woke he had put three rings on my fingers, made from bullets or the metal end of cartridge cases. 'Remember me,' he said like the ghost to Hamlet. Going on leave must have been almost worse than the trenches, if that was possible.

After this, the nearest I ever got to the real war, the indifference and incompetence of the hospital seemed worse than ever. It was as if nobody cared. Though we did not get the most ghastly casualties, what must have been in all these men's heads? The hospital had one good doctor whom all the English nurses loved. I never had the privilege of serving under him, but even he had an untroubled holiday attitude. Indeed there was a whole month in the summer when we had no patients at all. Perhaps during that month all the casualties were final.

When I revisited Houlgate after the war, it was packed with elegant and wealthy holiday makers. It was the family resort, highly decorous and stylish, like a Boudin painting. The more worldly Trouville-Deauville was a few miles away on one side, the demi-monde at Cabourg at a decent distance on the other. The whole coast hummed with activity and pleasure. Now it was deserted. A few villas were inhabited by the doctors and administrators, the rest shuttered up. During our enforced month's idleness the *Médecin-Chef* gave tea parties at his villa, the one admired doctor gave picnics on the Casino terrace, and Ary took me to his uncle's shooting lodge deep in the centre of Normandy, where in the woods there were wild boars. In the course of conversation he told me that when young men in the hospital asked him, '*Est-ce qu'il y a à faire avec Miss?*' he replied, '*Approchez-y, vous verrez.*' He had more faith in me than my mother.

Of course they approached. '*Si nous faisions une petite promenade ce soir?*'

One of my phobias, akin to uncompromising candour, was that words should be used for exactly what was meant, and that anybody approaching me must learn to do so. So when an evening walk was suggested it was with pleasure accepted. The unfortunate man found himself accompanying a brisk English stride for perhaps ten miles through the night and never even got to the point. Naturally no man ever confessed to this, but more probably boasted, so that I acquired a legendary bad name that nobody knew whether to believe or not. It is surprising that in spite of such idiocy I had some staunch female defenders. For the would-be amorous man I had a laughing but friendly contempt. There was no malice in my behaviour nor any aggressive ideas of Women's Lib. I thought I was proving my mother wrong again. Every girl must hold her own tiller.

In strong contrast to these wilful pranks I went to Paris for a weekend with Harold on leave from his chauffeuring. We stayed at the Crillon in the most elegant luxury. It still preserved its pre-war standards. I have no recollection of what I wore, but certainly it was not what those doors usually admitted. I was living free at the hospital and so had no money problems and Harold had a lieutenant's pay to spend on leave. We ate at various superb restaurants with famous names, and idled about the town and the Bois de Boulogne. At night we shared a bedroom fit for Ninon de Valois. The curtains, hanging from ceiling to floor, were of heavy damask whose glorious colour I can only describe as gold, but rich and deep. Played over by the dim bedside light it was beautiful enough to caress one's eyes all night. The bed curtains were the same. Everything was perfect, nothing was too much. The room closed us with exquisite voluptuousness.

We laid our young bodies together in this ambience as passionate as we were separate, no sword between us but an age old principle not yet questioned, no gesture but of dear trembling friendship, and we did not sleep for pure joy.

So great a trust engendered in me a love that was etched into my being, never to be erased. I was too ignorant to know that trust to this extent can be less perfect to the one trusted, could indeed cause love-hate. From now on I was from time to time subjected to slights and woundings that I could not understand. But I loved and had to take what was given. We met in Paris several times again, but found ourselves less ambassadorial lodging.

*

The hospital was ordered to make room for more wounded and so the nurses were turned out to find accommodation elsewhere. I was taken in by the *pharmacien* and his wife, free of charge again, as a patriotic gesture. They were good to me. The young wife was charming and of that willing correctness that the French do so beautifully. The house was faultlessly kept. I blush now to think what a shock I must have been to them. I should obviously have cleaned my own room but I had never cleaned a room and did not even realise it was necessary. My hostess never chided me, but if she ever looked in while I was out she saw a horrific mess. My night-gown too was an old frayed woollen shirt of Harold's with sleeves longer than my fingertips. My outdoor coat was one of his cast off mackintoshes, tattered and oily. If my morals were out of date my habits were two generations ahead. I would have been 'with it' now. While I was there, the wife's sister came to stay, bringing her son, a hefty two-year-old. His mother told me with pride that he was still breast fed. The little man in a sailor suit and so-called sailor hat was led in. As he was lifted on to her lap his mother said, '*Ote ton chapeau à ta petite maman, chéri.*'

*

The wards were busy again as summer drew towards autumn. I was glad to have work. Halcyon as my summer had been, the thought of the trenches was never absent. The one high-lighted the other. The patients never talked about it. They were not a talkative lot. They probably knew there were no words for it, at least to us. Perhaps they talked among themselves at night, or in the bistro if they could get there. All the time I was there, as far as I know not one had a visitor. Perhaps it was about now that the fat sergeant in the office, of whom I spoke at the beginning, told me that there was a patient who had to be escorted to his home in Alsace Lorraine. He was not strong enough to travel alone, no man could be spared to take him and none of the nurses would like to travel alone with a man. What about me? Of course I said I would. It delighted me to agree. I was the youngest by far and the least imposing of the nurses. That only made it more of a snook to pull. The journey was totally uneventful. I remember of it only the strange Alsatian countryside out of the railway window, like an illustration to fairy tales. Also that I spent the night in a hotel on the main street where my bedroom was on the ground floor. Being English I never slept with my windows shut, so I opened them—the tall glass doors, a very conspicuous sight in a French street, but not even a thief noticed. Men's voices loud in conversation passed on the pavement all night, but I was undisturbed.

The English nurse I saw most of had fallen in love with a classically featured young man from a farm in the Basses-Alpes. He had been badly wounded and could never do active

(129)

service again. She was older than he, too individual to be called plain, with vivid blue eyes in a long red face, and awkward but expressive movements. However, her face had the capacity of showing the intense despairing, fighting-for-life quality of her love. She had a quick sense of humour, but he had none. He was tired from the war, would not be able to pull his weight again on the farm and had no will to contend with her obsession. I watched him slowly and it seemed to me apprehensively drawn in. He had nothing to pit against her. When he was released from the hospital he agreed to marry her and went home to prepare his family and get his demobilisation papers.

In the lovely early autumn the bride and I set off for the Basses-Alpes. At the end of the long railway journey from Paris across the width of France we still had to travel half a day's ride in a carrier's open cart along small country roads. The scenery was bewitching, with the real Alps just visible beyond the rolling hills. I was so serenely happy taking it all in that I must have been poor company for my wildly agitated friend. We arrived at last, to find a small isolated farm on the top of a hill, and were received by an elder brother and his wife, and the bridegroom.

The room downstairs was the kitchen, where hens, ducks and goats ran about, the open door being the main light. The sister-in-law showed us her baby. It lay on her lap, its arms and legs trussed up in a tight criss-cross bundle as stiff as a log, as in early pictures. My friend and I shared a bedroom over the cow-shed. The floor boards were loosely fitted to allow the warmth of the animals to rise, as also the warm cow smell. Rustlings, sighs and low moos sweetened my sleep, but I daresay the bride's wakefulness was consoled by thoughts of the Surrey comforts she was offering him, poor boy. But what nostalgia he must later have suffered.

The wedding next day was only half a ceremony, conducted with ill grace by the priest because the bride was not a Catholic. He insisted that she must promise to bring up all

children in the faith if she was to be married at all. She said
she would say it aloud if it was all right to say inwardly that
she was sorry she did not mean it. The priest passed this over
without comment—she was only a mad English woman—and
married they were. We then had the wedding feast at a long
trestle table in a barn or village hall. The special dish in
honour of the occasion was a broiled calf's head, whole, and
of a ghastly whiteness like that of a dead human. The bride
and bridegroom were given the eyes. She disgraced herself by
refusing. I was let off lightly with the soft warm nostrils. The
men all ate with the jack knives out of their pockets which
they also used pertinaciously and openly for picking their
teeth, but knives and forks were found for us. I enjoyed the
Breughel atmosphere very much, and received an offer of
marriage from one of the guests before the end.

After the meal we formed up in procession and walked
from farm to farm over the hills for hours to show ourselves
to the neighbours, with much singing on the way.

That night I went off alone, seen off at the train by my
would-be husband who had driven me there in his float.

*

The ensuing winter was very severe. In my bedroom the
water in the ewer was frozen an inch deep every morning. It
is not surprising that we had a trainload of bronchitics. The
noise of coughing in the ward was like the hunt kennels before
feeding time. The echoes of it came down from the Casino
ceiling above the shrouded chandeliers. It was heard everywhere. The approved treatment—I guess originating from
Louis XIV's time—was cupping. I was shown how this
should be done. The patient lay with his back bared. I had
twelve small glass cups like very thick sherry glasses, into
which one at a time was put a tuft of cotton wool soaked in
methylated spirit and set on fire. While it was still flaming it
was clapped on to the flesh. If it was hot enough when put on,
the vacuum caused as it cooled drew up a red balloon from
the back inside it. If not hot enough, it fell off. To get a back

covered with these horrors took at least a quarter of an hour while the patient got cold. I cannot think it ever did any good. And how could a man lie down after it?

On the other hand, experimental medicine was going on. Someone had thought up that medicines swallowed sometimes upset the stomach. So the order went out that all medicines were to be given by hypodermic injections. I had till now never had an injection myself, still less used a hypodermic needle. I was nervous, having no idea how hard one would have to push it.

Injections in France were given in the buttock. Morning and evening all the men in my ward were drawn up facing a wall, their trousers down to their knees. An elderly French-woman had drifted in to help. She had armed herself with an instrument that perhaps was meant for drawing fluid out of the lung, a huge thing. With this she was stabbing the unfortunates. I managed to get a needle of sorts, lamentably blunt, and set to work. The scene was farcical, the old one with her prong, the young one with her needle, and my irresistible mirth spread to the whole row. It turned into a lark. When after two days the old lady withdrew and I had a little more confidence we settled down to a nearly professional routine, but solemn I could never be.

*

In the early spring I went on leave to England to meet Harold. I had the usual long day to pass in Le Havre by myself before the boat and felt far too excited to endure it. As I walked aimlessly about, I saw a group of four English officers sitting at a table outside a building. Spontaneously wrong, as usual, but moved by a feeling of our being all English in a war together, I went to their table and said simply, 'I haven't seen an Englishman for six months. May I sit and talk to you for a while? I'm waiting for the boat.'

At once the three nicest of the group rose and fled. The remaining man too got to his feet and said, 'Shall we go somewhere else? This is Headquarters.' I apologised. I didn't know the English were now established at Le Havre. He led me away, saying he knew a quiet place where we could go. It turned out to be a small hotel. The patronne greeted him as a valued client and said to my surprise, 'Your usual room, Monsieur'. We went upstairs, not to a salon but to a bedroom with a large double bed. No sooner were we inside than a maid came in and turned down the sheets at both sides. I began to laugh with real enjoyment of the ridiculousness, the ready speed of those turned down sheets. I explained that he had got it all wrong. I tried to convince him of the simplicity of my approach, but he could not believe it. I kept him off with the hot end of my cigarette and laughter without resentment. In the end he accepted defeat, saying as we parted at the hotel door, 'Well, you can't say I haven't behaved like a gentleman.' Rather touching, because he wasn't one at all.

So there was an afternoon passed with some interest and another lesson rubbed in. Alas, may one never behave naturally?

*

I do not clearly remember much about London that time except that we saw a Zeppelin caught in the searchlights over Wimbledon Common. We were visiting an aunt who was hysterical about the danger, clinging to her husband. Had it been the Second World War she would not have been so ridiculous, might perhaps even have been brave. The Zeppelin was brought down harmlessly except to the pilot.

The really sharp memory of this leave is the Alhambra, its galleries packed from first floor to ceiling with young officers in uniform, a sight to blink at, to try to take in and never forget. At the point the war had reached it was written as if on the wall that they must all be killed. The face of any young man who is fit and going arm in arm with death has a glory with its tragedy, and in the romantic light and excitement of the Alhambra there they all were, some remembering what they came from too vividly to laugh, some even more tense in the effort to forget. Enough to choke a girl's heart. These were my real English.

In the stalls where I sat in full view of this reredos of those ready to die, I was abandoned by Harold who left me for the Promenade, improper for 'ladies', where he said he would meet other old friends. So there I sat throughout the show, alone in a non-world of my own making with an empty stall beside me, and took in the totality. Meanwhile Robey was singing 'If you were the only girl in the world', a song of bitter-sweet truth for us all.

*

Back once more in Houlgate I found the hotel where the nurses had once lodged was now given over to tubercular patients. My ward in the Casino had only a few wounded who had lingered on, so I had little to do. A large room opening out of it had eight or ten men said to be tubercular. They were being subjected to an experimental treatment. They were encased in plaster from neck to ankles, leaving only their arms free, and their feet sticking out at the end. Each man, as he could not move his head, had a small tilted looking glass above his face so that he could see something besides the ceiling. I was asked, as I had time on my hands, to massage their feet. Of course I had no training in massage but was not likely to do any harm, so I made it as long and pleasant as I could while talking to these medical martyrs via their mirror. It was a room that horrified me, but I never heard a grumble from them. The way they took whatever was ordained was astounding, for it must have occurred to them that this treatment was medical lunacy. They died one by one, not of their disease but of dreadful bedsores, which might have been foreseen. My Scottish Nanny was shocked beyond comment.

*

About this time my brother Phil was reported missing. His plane had been shot down. This may very well have shocked Harold into further action for I learned from his letters that he had offered himself for the Flying Corps, where in the growing shortage of men, his lameness was not considered a serious handicap, and he was taken on. He had been sent to a training centre outside Tours, whence I received enthusiastic accounts of his new made friends. His men friends were always for life. Needless to say, in midsummer I went to visit him, in a part of France new to me, but of which I actually saw very little. I put up in a small hotel, which had a pleasant balcony overlooking open spaces and trees, where meals were served. But it was not Harold who shared it. He could only get away for a couple of hours in the evening, after which he returned to camp. We sat on a bench at the edge of a wood overlooking the town and he talked to me about the new and wonderful Bristol Moth, and about his friends, but was always careful to keep them away from me. But my constant companion, arriving even at breakfast time, was a young Canadian flyer who managed to get away from camp more enthusiastically than Harold and was deluded enough to think I would make the ideal wife for a trapper, which was his peacetime occupation. He saw me going round with him to get the fur—not the poor creature—out of his nightly traps. Otherwise he was a nice boy and had got it badly, for the moment. Marriage was in the air. At Houlgate there was a little village baker, as good as gold, who was now the hospital ambulance driver. He offered to teach me to drive. He took his engine to pieces to show me how it worked and explained very clearly, while he and I put it together again. The ambulance was kept in a small yard behind a restaurant. The yard was lined with cages of rabbits stacked one above the other all round. In this very cramped space he made me use all the gears and turn the car completely round in short zig-zags. Under his placid common-sense tuition it seemed easy. I did it without startling a rabbit. After that he arranged that I should walk a good way out of possible observation from the hospital where he would pick me up in his cab and I should drive the wounded into Trouville. I do not think I shook a patient, but of course we were the only car on the road. In return for these lessons I began to teach him English, sitting at a table in my bedroom. He had very formal manners. Alas, one day he arrived in his best clothes with a neat little posy of flowers, to offer me his heart. There were no more lessons. Much later when I first drove Harold's car with himself beside me, at a bad change of gear up a very steep hill he so hissed through his teeth that I lost my nerve and took him straight into a fruit shop among flying oranges and apples. For him driving was a religious exercise. The engine was the divinity.

To come back to Tours, Harold had the weekend off and arranged to meet me at a tiny place called Gué de Loire, where there was a riverside inn. He borrowed a bicycle for me and promised to meet me at midday. I rode off happily for what seemed a very great way, through vineyard country most strange to me as the vines were painted brilliant blue. I do not think I met anyone all the way there. I arrived at last at an idyllic place and took a room at the inn, then sat down to wait for Harold. Hour after hour passed and he did not come. I had a lonely lunch, and finally in tears a lonely supper under the suspicious eye of the landlady who obviously thought that if my man was dropping me I should not be able to pay the bill and so must not be allowed out of sight. I suffered great humiliation but at last as it was growing dark he arrived, with a believable excuse. I chose to believe it, and friendship was restored. Next day the weather was brilliant. We spent the morning lying on a hillside in the sun in great content to be in such a country, and the afternoon bathing in a little river that ran beneath over-arching trees. Above the water hung a loose bluish haze, made of dragonflies' wings that flashed in the sun-specks as they hovered and darted in great numbers.

Though it had its charming moments this brief visit did not advance our affair at all. Harold's conversation had been largely about his new friends, one in particular who was having a love affair with a local girl. Harold found it very entertaining to see his friend hampered and guilty because he had a wife in England who 'absolutely idolised him'. I saw nothing funny in it and said I would rather be a mistress treated with frankness than a wife treated with deceit. It did not occur to me that a ladylove could be treated with as much or more deceit than a wife, only a man would not be bothered by it.

*

When I got back to Houlgate, I was told that Ary was leaving. He had been posted to Paris. He came to say goodbye to me, looking very white. He had looked ill for some time. I thought it was with breathing too much chloroform. His clothes always smelled of it. I was sorry to lose him. 'Ary, do you really have to go?'

'*Je l'ai demandé moi-même. Ah, Miss, c'est que je vous aime mieux que Dieu. Ainsi il faut que je m'en aille.*'

Such a confession commands entire respect. I have never made light of Ary.

The hospital was growing dreary. My two best friends had gone, as also my Scottish Nanny. The surgical side was closing down. The hotels were full of the tubercular. No treatment was then known for tuberculosis but the amelioration of fresh air and good food. I doubt if their diet was enlarged. Certainly they had no fresh air. I once had to go through the hotel looking for one of the nurses. Each room all along the corridors had four men in it with the windows tightly closed. They just sat there with nothing to do or think about till they died, which they did each in his turn, and were taken to the dying cupboard. The hospital had become a dying-house, quite as a matter of course. In the trenches or here, what did it matter? I admit I was not nursing them so can only give my impression.

Of course at any moment it might be changed. They might send us a trainload of typhoid. We hadn't had that yet.

My thoughts must at this time have been elsewhere, for I remember very little of what I did. I had at least one serious

(137)

case to look after and was beginning to feel a little more confidence in myself as a nurse. I went now for company to the office in the Casino, where the old sergeant and the gentleman seemed equally short of occupation. The sergeant amused himself, as the men had so often done, in trying to shock me, but he went much further. He went a very long way, with the most outrageous Rabelaisian grossness that must have pained his reserved and proper colleague. All ran off me like water off a duck's back. I understood it, and I understood him, I was simply interested in what could be said. It fascinated the old man, but had he succeeded in offending me, he would have been miserable.

*

In September Harold wrote that he was back in England, at Portmeadow in Oxford, finishing his very brief training before going to the front. If I wanted to see him I must come soon. Off I went, and he met me in London. We went to the current reviews, Violette Lorraine and George Robey still our favourites. The songs of the time were woven into the fabric of our being as I think the current songs always are for each generation of the young, but then they were ennobled by the omnipresence of death. It puts a size and an edge on everything.

The imminence of the front rocked our established if abnormal relationship. The last night I found my face being covered with kisses the whole night through, hour after hour till it was perforated and smarting from the morning's bristles. When it was time to leave me he sighed, 'Aren't you *ever* going to marry me?'

I think I may have said something like Perhaps; but marriage had never before been mentioned. I did not know if his question was rhetorical or the *sincerité du moment*, or real. He got up then, put on his Flying Corps uniform on which I had sewn the wings, and we parted.

I went back to Houlgate in a daze, but once there my mind was clear. For God's sake, instead of all this death, let us have some life. If a man only wanted to have an heir to his name, would I refuse? I ardently wanted to be given this to do for him. I sent a telegram saying Yes, and proceeded to pack up and close my connection with the hospital. In a very short time I was back.

*

Portmeadow was a romantic setting near the tiny village of Wolvercote, which consisted of a few cottages, a church and the Trout Inn. The inn stood beside the river at the foot of a bridge. A narrow stream divided it from an island which now was covered with white bell tents, looking, especially by moonlight, like a mediaeval picture of a battle confrontation. This was where the pilots slept. The Trout too was like something out of Chaucer, so remote and simple, but the landlady could cook. Before the war it may have been a place where parties from Oxford came for supper, taking the long walk across Portmeadow. If it had a bar, it must have been somewhere at the back. I never noticed it. No crowds of officers came to drink there, no local merriment was heard at night. I seemed to be quite alone. The strip of riverbank outside the inn door was so neglected it had turned into a series of ivy grottos, one of which had a bench where I could sit and listen to the roar of water under the bridge. The omnipresent noise isolated me from the sounds of the camp, though so near. A narrow plank bridge crossed from the island to the inn, but no one crossed it except Harold.

Inside the inn there was a good deal of noise at night. The innkeeper was a drunkard and perhaps bedridden. From his bedroom he bombarded his wife with bottles thrown at random down the stairs accompanied by ravings. But this forsaken and down-going place was my love and sanctuary. I could imagine nowhere I would sooner be.

We had decided to get married by special licence at once, and as privately as possible. I sent a telegram to Mother to tell her.

Two pieces of advice were offered me at this turning point. The old landlady hung over me watchfully.

'Don't you give him what he wants before you're married, dearie. Take my advice. *Don't do it*. It's always a mistake.' She couldn't keep it in, it seemed to touch her closely.

Mother sent Mary post haste down to Oxford to bring me a message. I met her in the Mitre and she stayed only long enough to deliver it. She was embarrassed and could not find words that she could bring herself to say. She grew red and scratched herself, but finally brought out,

'Mother says, if it's for *that*, don't.'

But, as usual, I did.